Feng Shui

FOR YOUR HOME

SARAH SHURETY

RIDER

London · Sydney · Auckland · Johannesburg

I wish to thank my sister Elizabeth and all my precious family, past and present, including my best friend Rowland, and all the many people who have come into my life and taught me different facets of feng shui.

And a very special thank you to Jane Alexander and everyone at Random House who have helped bring feng shui to people all over the world.
Thank you also to Mandy Francis and Paul Wolfenden.

I would particularly like to dedicate this book to the memory of all the feng shui masters who died in the cultural revolution.

First published in 1997

9 10 8

Text copyright © Sarah Shurety 1997
Special illustrations © Michael Hill 1997

Sarah Shurety has asserted her right to be identified as the author of this work in accordance with the Copyright, Designs and Patents Act, 1988.

First published in the United Kingdom in 1997 by Rider
an imprint of Ebury Press
Random House · 20 Vauxhall Bridge Road · London SW1V 2SA

Random House Australia (Pty) Limited
20 Alfred Street · Milsons Point · Sydney · New South Wales 2061 · Australia

Random House New Zealand Limited
18 Poland Road · Glenfield · Auckland 10 · New Zealand

Random House South Africa (Pty) Limited
Endulini, 5A Jubilee Road, Parktown 2193, South Africa

The Random House Group Limited Reg. No. 954009

www.randomhouse.co.uk

A CIP catalogue record for this book is available from the British Library.

ISBN 0 7126 7102 1

Edited by Emma Callery
Designed by Lovelock & Co.
Picture research by Nadine Bazar
Illustrations by Michael Hill

Printed and bound in Portugal by Printer Portuguesa, Lisbon

Contents

Part I: Introducing feng shui   4

Introduction   7
What is feng shui?   8
Clutter   14
The bagua   18

Part II: Applying feng shui   30

The entrance to your world   32
Sitting rooms   44
Kitchens   50
Dining rooms   56
Bedrooms   62
Children's rooms   76

Bathrooms and toilets   82
Studies   88
Gardens   94
Choosing a new home   100

Part III: Refining your feng shui skills   106

The nine basic cures   108
Cleansing   126
Directionology   132
The flying stars   136

Useful addresses   139
Further reading   139
Acknowledgments   139
Index   140

Introducing feng shui

Introduction

Have you ever noticed how, when you lived in one home, your life was very happy but when you moved to another house, or built an extension, everything started to go wrong? As an exercise, think about your home right now. Close your eyes and picture it: what does it feel like? how do you feel about it? Your home is an extension of you and whatever you are feeling, and so your home in some way reflects what is happening in your life at the moment.

You have selected your home and everything in it from the carpets to the ornaments. Even with articles that were gifts, you decide where to put them, whether to hide them in the attic or display them on top of the mantelpiece. Is there an area of your house that is always dark and cluttered? If so, that area will relate to some aspect of yourself that is also dark and cluttered (at the moment). Your home is a constantly changing reflection of your life, so whatever changes you make in your home, you make to yourself.

Although we all have our own separate fields of energy, we are all linked together and everything around us, animate and inanimate, has an influence. Feng shui's aim is to balance all these energies to ensure that we are harmoniously in accord with the universe so that the energy in our immediate surroundings, internally and externally can be as supportive as possible.

Feng shui originated in China some 3,000 years ago, but since the 1950s, by a strange twist of fate, it has been officially banned there. Mao Tse Tung decided it was not an acceptable discipline and destroyed all the manuscripts he could find and imprisoned or punished all feng shui masters. Despite his attempts, though, Chairman Mao could not eliminate feng shui and to this day it is still widely practised in China, but with discretion.

In the other countries of the East, feng shui is used as an essential part of life. When Western entrepreneurs set up business branches in Hong Kong, Singapore and parts of Malaysia, they had to use feng shui. This was because the local people put up a united front and simply refused to work in a building unless it had been approved by a feng shui consultant, which shows a phenomenal belief. Westerners gradually came to appreciate its benefits and the science has slowly travelled across the oceans to be used all over the world. Read this book to learn more about the subject, and you too will discover how to fill your life and home with health, wealth and happiness.

opposite: Mirrors are like a virtual reality. They bring more energy into an area.

What is feng shui?

The trigrams from

The I Ching

Kan, meaning Water

Kun, meaning Earth

Zhen, meaning Thunder

Sun, meaning Wind

Qian, meaning Heaven

Dui, meaning Lake

Gen, meaning Mountain

Li, meaning Fire

Feng shui may sound like an obscure Chinese dish but literally translated it means 'wind and water'. Feng (pronounced foong) means wind. Shui (pronounced shway) means water, and water is an analogy for wealth.

It all began a long time ago with a turtle. Between 2953 and 2838 BC, to be exact, a great Emperor called Fu Hsi was sitting by the banks of the river Lo enjoying the sunshine, when he noticed a turtle ponderously climbing ashore. The turtle symbolises the universe. Its dome-shaped back represents the skies, and its shell, covered with various markings, echoes the constellations and the planets. Its belly is comparable to the earth, and the turtle moves through the water in a similar fashion to the way the land is surrounded by the great oceans. The turtle or tortoise is known as one of the four 'spiritually endowed' creatures (the unicorn, phoenix and dragon are the other three, see the seventh cure, page 118). The turtle is recorded in the *Records of Science* as living to an age of 1,000 years, so he has become a symbol of longevity, strength, endurance and wisdom.

As Fu Hsi regarded the turtle with all this in his mind, he looked long and hard at the markings on its back. The patterns seemed to change as the sun dried the shell and suddenly he had a flash of inspiration and saw the markings as the trigrams that you can find in the I Ching (see illustration, left). From these trigrams he made up the lo shu or magic square. The lo shu is another name for the bagua that is the template which is laid over the plan of a property to establish which area of the building relates to which aspect of your life (see pages 18-29).

For the first two or three thousand years of feng shui's existence, its main application was to site a grave for the dead: to choose an auspicious day for burial, the best orientation and a good location. Ancient people did not need to consult someone about the feng shui of a building for the living because they lived so closely to nature. Their lives were governed by the seasons and they lived in harmony with the natural rhythms of the world, understanding its rules and cycles. They intuitively knew that they should not build their houses in certain places.

Modern people, however, have become so cocooned from nature that their intuition is not so strong and they no longer understand how the universe functions. Most of us have experienced times during the winter when we have to get up in the dark, work all day in an artificially lit environment, and then come home, again in the dark, and we wouldn't have had a clue about what was happening in the garden. This can result in such an imbalance in your intuition that you can end up thinking how wonderful it would be to live on the edge of a cliff, with a wonderful view of the sea. This, however, would not be good since the chances of your building eventually slipping into the sea would be quite high, and normally your common sense would have told you that.

It is said that a part of the spirit called the 'po' resides with the mortal remains for at least four years after someone has passed on. The bones are very important because they are believed to resonate like crystals. They are genetically unique so it is possible for a scientist to identify which bones are from a relative and which from a stranger. According to the Chinese, you are linked to your ancestors for seven generations and so the siting of the grave is very important.

You may be able to relate to this link by thinking of your mother. For example, when she is really worried or unhappy you will feel a bit anxious or unhappy yourself. If she is very happy you will somehow feel more contented. Every culture has a similar view. The Bible refers to this link when it says 'the sins of the father will be visited on the son for the next seven generations'. This is not referring to the sins of pillaging and plundering, but to the sin of not having looked after yourself well enough so that when you pass on you may not have enough energy to get to the next level. If you get stuck, you are a bit miserable, and if any of our ancestors or relatives are miserable, then so are we.

Feng shui has been used in China for more than 3,000 years to position buildings and burial sites. Here, a Chinese temple has a protective mountain behind it.

If you have a child, you may have found that somehow you knew when they were tangled in a sheet and needed you, or when something was wrong at school. This is often referred to as 'having a sixth sense'. If your child grows up and goes to live far away and you lose touch, you will still have a feeling of how they are.

In feng shui, we believe you are also responsible for the next seven generations to come. This means that even if you don't have any children but your sister does, then in some way you are responsible for her children and your happiness is interlinked. By looking after your family you are looking after yourself. If a member falls by the wayside, then so do we.

Surveying the plot

A feng shui master, or feng shui hsien-sheng, will often have among his equipment something called a luo pan (or compass), which means a dish in which you can see everything in the world. In the early days, the compass was just a lodestone (magnetised rock) with an iron spoon that would spin round to point to magnetic north. The handle pointed towards the north and the dish part to the south to establish which way the sun would rise. The Chinese were the first to invent the compass and they called it 'the south pointing chariot'. The luo pan comprises many rings and the trigrams of the I Ching are marked on the first two rings. The first ring represents the pre-heaven sequence (that described by Fu Hsi) and the second ring, the post-heaven sequence (an amended positioning of the trigrams with human beings at the centre). The luo pan is made to special dimensions, and it is often used as a powerful cure to repel shas (malignant, threatening forms of chi).

This would be a perfect site on which to build a village, with the mountains behind indicating the strong energy of the site.

The first thing a feng shui master does is to examine the terrain. He sees which areas become boggy in the winter, which way the trees have bent (to give an indication of the prevalent winds), and where the grass is greenest. He then looks at the locations of the mountains and the rivers, noting the points the river reaches during the highest tides, and the direction in which it flows.

At the heart of the earth is a magnetic core of molten iron, and radiating from it are strong currents of energy which are known as dragon veins. As they force their way through the earth with a tremendous power, something akin to a pressure cooker releasing steam, they contribute to the creation of mountains and the general terrain. Mountains can be seen as an expression of the type of energy found in that area. As the energy lessens and time passes, with the help of the weather, the mountains soften into hills, and then mounds. From the shape of the mountain and its age, a feng shui master can determine what kind of energy is diffusing the immediate area. The strongest dragon veins are indicated by the biggest mountains and these energies are always in motion with the dragon veins continually finding different outlets, constantly shifting and changing the energy of the world.

Spirits move around either in ley lines, through electricity or through the energy fields of living things. A feng shui master can tell what kind of energy each dragon vein has and can therefore establish what would be the most suitable application for a plot. He can determine whether it would be an appropriate place to site a building, and which direction would be most auspicious for the front door, the bedroom and such like.

To feel the energy of the site, the feng shui master walks around, pausing occasionally and using his body as a compass. We all do this. I'm sure you have walked into a house and thought, 'this is nice and cosy', and at other times thought, 'I don't like it here at all.' You are using your senses to 'feel' the atmosphere. You can refine these senses and find that each room of your home has a different ambience. People often find that they have favourite rooms for reading the newspapers and another one for chatting with friends. The feng shui master has refined these senses through practice to such a degree that by just walking around the plot he can feel what sort of energy is coming up from the earth.

Chi and its different forms

To further understand the concept of feng shui we need to understand more about energy, or 'chi'. As already touched on, everything in the universe has an energy field unique to itself, but influenced and linked in some way to everything else. Likewise, everything has a 'flow', like a river that flows down to the sea. When we are sailing in this direction we can make great headway and it is easy, but, when we try to go against the current and sail up-stream, life becomes much more difficult. Correspondingly, when we are correctly and harmoniously positioned in the universe, whether at home or at work, we have both balance and harmony. We are flowing with the powerful workings of nature, and our health, prosperity and mental state benefit. Conversely, when we are out of step with the natural rhythms of the universe, our lives can be a constant struggle, just like the boat going against the current.

Heaven's chi

This is the chi from the planets and constellations. The energy emanating from the full moon gives people more energy. If you throw a party when the moon is full, it will go with much more zest; unfortunately accidents and crime rates increase, too. It also regulates women's menstrual cycles. When the planets make up certain configurations, the weather can seem unusual, whales may beach themselves, birds migrate, and insects and people behave in an erratic fashion.

Man-made chi

Another form of energy is man-made. If you work in a building that has sealed windows and air conditioning, lots of electrical equipment, synthetic carpets and wall coverings, you will feel an influence from the atmosphere. In a building that has an indoor fountain, lots of plants, an open fire and views across the countryside, you will feel completely different.

The chi of living things

If I were to release a little mouse into the room and it ran rapidly hither and thither you would find that your heart would start to beat a little faster and your energy would resonate with the small but intense energy field of the mouse. Conversely, if a tortoise was to ponderously walk into the garden, and you remained sitting in your chair and watched him, you would feel your heartbeat slow down and you would start to resonate with the tortoise's energy and become ponderous and slow yourself.

The country's chi

Where you live in the world will dictate to some extent your personality. If you live in a cold, grey climate, it will make your temperament a bit colder. This is partly linked to your health because if you live in a damp, grey environment you are likely to suffer from what traditional Chinese medicine calls a 'damp condition'. This means that energy does not move fast and among the symptoms are stagnation, depression (depression comes from not expressing), stubbornness (which comes from non-movement), and steadiness. If you live in a hot, tropical climate that is disposed to sudden dramatic changes in the weather it will make you more tempestuous, so people tend to be more excitable, passionate, changeable and demonstrative (see also the flying stars, pages 136-39).

Cities and villages also have their own chi. Hence you will find one part of a city may have the energy to support or influence people to become bankers, and a financial centre will spring up. If an entrepreneur decides to set up a clothing shop in that area it probably will not thrive because the energy is not supportive to that sort of industry.

Predecessor chi

Most of us know of a high street shop that keeps changing hands and each time to a different sort of business. But no matter how enthusiastic the new proprietor is, after a short time the business folds. History tends to repeat because of the predecessor chi that is created by people walking backwards and forwards in the building for years on end leaving an energy imprint. When you move in, you start to absorb some of this chi that tends to make the history of that house repeat. Whatever has happened to the previous tenants is an indication of what is likely to happen to you. You need to be especially careful

Incidents of predecessor chi

The dog who ran away

I once gave a consultation in a house in Hampstead. A young mother answered the door and a lovely black dog shot past me and bounded off across the heath. The house had an air of happy confusion. The family lived in the house happily until they had another baby. then they moved to a bigger house. Some years later, I had a request for a consultation at the same address. I arrived, knocked at the door and when a young mother answered, a yellow Labrador shot past me and bounded off across the heath. There was also the same atmosphere of happy confusion and the family were planning another child.

John

The flat to the other side of me, which was much bigger, had a single gentleman living in it. He moved there with his young wife but after only a year they quarrelled, she moved, and he lived there for the next ten years on his own. They had purchased the flat from a single man who had lived there for about 15 years. He had also originally moved in with his new wife but they had separated and she had left him after only a year and a half. John, still single, decided to sell the flat and a young couple who had just become engaged bought it, but within six months they quarrelled and he moved out leaving her on her own.

if the predecessor chi of fire has occurred in a property more than once, as this is a strong indication that the building is prone to fire.

If you want to get rid of the predecessor chi in your home, often a simple cure (see pages 108-25) will correct the problem that began the chain of events. But the energetic vibration, say of stress and depression, left behind by the previous tenants compounds the problem and the building will usually need to be cleansed (see pages 126-29).

A feng shui consultation

There are many different schools of feng shui (see page 18), but if you have a consultation you can usually expect to begin with a discussion about your aims and any sensitive issues you are concerned about. The consultant will generally ask you when you moved into the building, the date the building was completed, and from which direction you travelled (see Directionology, pages 132-5). He will ask you how long you were at the previous residence to establish how your energy is and about the history of the building – or the predecessor chi. If you are thinking of moving house, you will be advised which are your most auspicious directions and what will be likely to happen if you move in that direction, and what would be the best date to do it. If you are about to go on an important trip, the consultant will advise you of the best dates to go and in what direction you should be travelling. He will warn you about any years of rest or low intuition and most will also give you the best dates to launch a new business, get married, or even start a book.

Next the consultant will survey the plot, whether it is your home or your office, and advise you what you need to do. This can be anything from simple furniture re-arrangement to building walls or closing up windows.

Clutter

The first rule of feng shui is no clutter. This is such an important facet of feng shui and such a problem of the twentieth century that I have devoted a whole chapter to the subject. If you want to use or apply feng shui, you will need to start with clutter.

Before you let anything into your life, you have to let something go. So before you apply any feng shui cures (see pages 108-25) you need to start by tidying up, cleaning and letting some things go. When energy can't flow easily, it stagnates. Clutter creates stagnation and makes everything grind to a halt, it makes you feel depressed, tired and stuck. If an area of your house is blocked and stagnant at the moment, this will be having a negative influence on the corresponding area of your life.

Whenever I am starting a new project, I have to give my house a spring clean as this allows me to think more clearly. Likewise, if I am feeling depressed, I clear out a cupboard. Clearing clutter releases huge amounts of positive energy and lifts your spirits. Whatever you are doing on the outside, you are also doing on the inside. So by clearing clutter you can let

This room, though neat and orderly, has too much clutter which can make you feel tired and blocked.

go of all sorts of negative emotions. I thoroughly enjoy throwing things out, and I promise you, that once you start the habit, you will too. Occasionally I have got carried away and last time I threw out my ironing board, but I may have been a little overzealous that time!

How can you tell whether you have too much clutter? If all week you have had the thought at the back of your mind that you must clear out that kitchen drawer or the back room, you have too much clutter. If whenever you think of your home you have a mental image of overstuffed cupboards and if tidying up generally involves making piles of things and moving them from one place to another, you have too much clutter. If the first thing you do with your precious spare time is tidy up, the clutter is too much. If even thinking about it makes you tired and the activity takes up the whole of your weekend, you have too much clutter.

It's a funny thing, but if you are one of those people who cannot let anything go because 'it might be useful one day', then you are sending out a message that you do not trust the world to supply everything you need. Instead of becoming more secure, the opposite starts to happen and you become more insecure.

One of my clients was just this sort of person. She had a consultation and was inspired to thoroughly spring clean and throw out all the things she didn't need. During her massive de-cluttering programme she threw out an ancient tent that she had not used for twenty years. She rang me the next weekend quite cross because she had suddenly found she needed the tent. I suggested she bought one from a local newspaper and told her I would be happy to pay for it. She telephoned me a couple of weeks later to say she had bought a beautiful modern tent, far superior to the one she had discarded. She used it for the weekend, and then sold it the following week through the local paper for more than she had paid for it. And further more, she was happy with the thought that if she ever needed one again she could go through the same process without having to store it for twenty years. Not only had she made a profit and stayed in a beautiful spacious tent, but she had also broken the pattern of a lifetime. The universal law says that if you let something go, something else will come in.

You need to be balanced about your clutter. I find that when I am in the middle of a project, I accumulate masses of reference material, paper and such like and it helps to inspire new ideas. But when I have finished, my housecleaner and I do a big clear out so that it is all fresh to start the next day. Houses where people are neurotically tidy can become sterile places where you cannot 'breathe' and this can be as debilitating as being in a very cluttered one.

When I first got completely on top of my clutter and I was luxuriating in my new found clarity and tranquillity, my partner moved in bringing all his clutter with him –

> *There is a Japanese word called 'ma': it refers to the beauty of the space between objects.*

The chairs in this room have been arranged in a harmonious circle to ease the flow of conversation.

mountaineering gear including tents, ice picks and crampons, all his clothes and even his favourite armchair. I had still not managed to let go of the clutter in my mind so I had created him to bring it in physically. If this happens to you, you need to teach those people about clutter. I have taught workshops on cleansing and clearing out clutter and have often found that a student has sent their partner or children along to the next one so that everyone can feel equally inspired to de-clutter!

And finally Clutter is also that phone call you don't want to make, for as long as you put it off, it eats away at your energy while you think, 'Oh no, I don't want to ring so and so.' If you receive an exorbitant bill and you decide to make them wait, all the time you are waiting, you'll be thinking, 'I've been charged too much', and again it eats your energy. Much better to pay it straight away so that you can move on to other things with a clear mind. Letters that you owe – write them straight away, you'll feel much lighter. Things that are broken will irritate you every time you see them, so repair them or throw them out.

The wardrobe

Do you have so many clothes and shoes that you keep forgetting what you have in your wardrobe? If you have, this will often mean that when you are going out for a special occasion and can't decide what you want to wear, you pull out everything, make a big mess of your bedroom and then have to put it all back again. Looking after this many clothes makes you tired. Are you lucky enough to remember a time when you only had a couple of suits and a few pairs of jeans? If you do, you will also remember being absolutely clear about what you were going to wear and finding it very easy to keep tidy.

You do not need more than seven pairs of socks. If they start to go grey, throw them out and buy some more. If you are going to a ball, hire an evening dress. If you are going to a wedding, hire a hat. Those shoes that you have not worn for five years – throw them out. Take on the maxim 'something in, something out'.

Clutter in the car

I do a lot of mileage and sometimes spend as much as eight hours a day in the car. When this happens, you start to live in the car, eating, writing, charging your mobile phone, doing your hair and makeup, keeping a toothbrush, a change of footwear, hundreds of cassettes. Gradually your car becomes a mobile dustbin and whenever someone sees the inside of it you cringe with embarrassment and, guess what? This is an energy drain, so whenever you have finished with those talking books, give them away, get yourself a little hold-all for your bits and pieces, and clean the car regularly. You will feel much fresher.

Getting started

It is hard to win the 'clutter' battle, it seems to be the 'disease' of the twentieth century. But as soon as you let something go, something new comes in, so give it no quarter and learn to enjoy letting go.

If you are finding it difficult to start letting things go, use this transcendental cure. Move 27 things in your house that have not been moved for a long time every day for nine days, then start with something small and complete like a kitchen or bedroom drawer. Or throw one thing out every day, even if this is just an old toothbrush.

What's in your pockets?

Look in your pockets right now. What have you got? Sweet wrappers, nut shells and crumbs from when you last fed the squirrels or horses, and old receipts? Are you one of these people who, as you tidy the house, puts odd things into your pockets? This is still clutter, so empty all your pockets and start again.

The bagua

The place where you have the most control over the influence of the internal feng shui is in your home or office. Each different area in your home relates to a different aspect of your life and by making subtle changes to each room you can have a positive influence on that facet of your life.

Concepts from a culture that is very different from our own, like feng shui, can seem difficult to comprehend. You need to put aside all your pre-conceived ideas and go forward with an open mind in order to understand it. So let's begin.

There is an expression in China that says in life there are three things that can forecast the future. First there is destiny, then there is feng shui, and lastly there is luck. Destiny is mapped out for you, you were born with a certain nature, and you are likely to react to events in a predictable fashion and it therefore follows that your life can be predicted. You cannot change your nature or your destiny, but feng shui makes the most of what you have. It makes sure you are facing the right direction, doing the right thing at the right time in the right place, and thereby making the most of your luck. And finally, there is plain old luck, which is when you happen to be facing the right direction at the right time and doing the right thing by chance.

A statue of Jizo with money that has been given to bring good luck to all children.

The schools of feng shui

Feng shui is not an absolute science so there are many different schools, but the principle methods are The Compass School and the Classical Landscape Form School (often known simply as the Form School). The Form School is the oldest and many aspects are logical and filled with common sense that can be easily understood by anyone. The Compass School is very precise and uses dates of birth and configurations of the constellations in order to choose the most auspicious orientations. If the front door is facing a hill, according to the Form School, it cannot be auspicious and the resident will always face difficulties even if the orientation according to the Compass School is perfect, unless of course the hill were removed. So the Compass School will bow to the Form School and the second best direction would be chosen. In this book, I am going to look mainly at the aspects of the Form School.

Understanding the bagua

In feng shui, we believe that there are nine principal aspects to your life and to be really happy you need to have a good balance in each. These are the areas of the bagua (bagua means eight houses) that were derived from Fu Hsi's lo shu (see page 8) and they are: career, relationship, ancestors, wealth, health, benefactors, children, knowledge and fame (see the illustration, below). If you pay too much attention to your finances, your relationships, knowledge and health can suffer. If you pay too much attention to your children, your finances and your relationship with your spouse can suffer. And so on. Feng shui seeks a balance between all nine. Each relates to a different part of your house, facet of your life, a number, an organ in the body, a planet, and a season and a time when the energy is strongest. By placing the bagua template on your home or office you can establish how to improve the feng shui of each aspect. Then, by making subtle changes in any or all of those areas you can have a positive influence on those aspects of your life.

4	9	2
3	5	7
8	I	6

Wealth	Fame	Relationship
Ancestors	Health	Children
Knowledge	Career	Benefactors

Above is the lo shu or magic square from which the areas of the bagua template (right) were developed.

19

Relating the bagua to your home

To identify which area of your home relates to which aspect of your life you need to lay a template of the bagua over a plan of your home. The bagua template is always laid in such a way that the front door will fall in the career, benefactors or knowledge area. It doesn't matter which direction your house is facing, because most of the energy comes in through the front door – the mouth of chi – so this is your starting point. Your front door is the one that the postman uses and that which visitors automatically come to.

The bagua can be applied to any floor of your house or flat and if you live in a single-room flat, it can be applied to that room alone. Some schools of feng shui apply the bagua

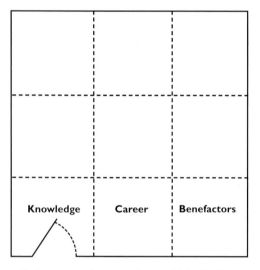

The bagua template is used to establish which area of your home relates to which area of your life.

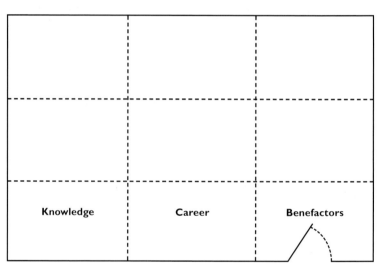

The bagua template is flexible and can be fitted over any shaped home.

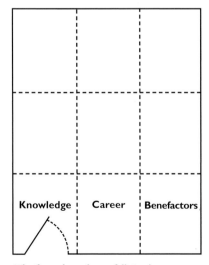

The front door always falls in the knowledge, career or benefactors area. In this instance, it falls in the knowledge area.

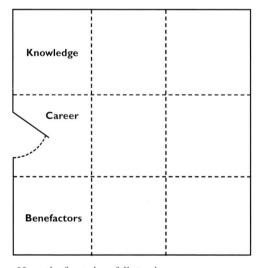

Here, the front door falls in the career area.

to each room as well as to the whole house, but I feel it should only be applied to the whole house otherwise you can become neurotic. The exception would be children's rooms because these rooms can be thought of as their own homes (see suggested area cures on page 81).

Start by laying the bagua over the ground floor plan of your house. If you don't already have a ground floor plan, draw one onto squared paper making sure you draw it accurately. Mark all doors and windows onto the plan. Lay the bagua onto the plan so that the career, benefactors and knowledge areas fall along the wall that includes your front door. To accommodate houses that are of different proportions to the bagua, you can amend the shape of the bagua, as shown below.

Discovering missing and extended areas

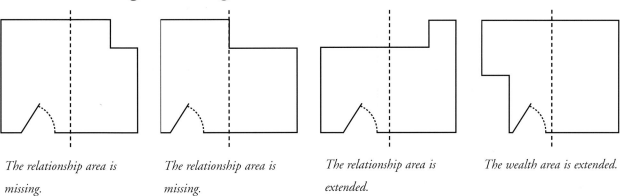

The relationship area is missing.

The relationship area is missing.

The relationship area is extended.

The wealth area is extended.

Once you have applied the bagua you may find that you have missing or extended areas. To establish whether an area is missing or extended, mentally draw a line down the centre of your home. (If you have a plan, you can do this physically on the plan.) If the area missing is equal or less than half, it is regarded as a missing area. If the area missing is greater than half, what remains is an extension (see above).

When the bagua template is applied to the upper floor, regard the top step as the mouth of chi. Most of the energy on the upper levels generally comes up from the stairs. So lay the template against the top step, and then drag it back to the exterior wall of your property (or the last wall belonging to your flat). Then you can clearly recognise which areas are which. This is not a rule etched in stone, however. Over time you will come to use your body as a compass and you will find that in some houses the energy repeats the same energy pattern of the ground floor, while others are quite different.

Area number 1: the career area

Most of the energy or opportunity in the house comes in through the front door so the career area is always found near this portal. Even if it opens into the Benefactors area it will still affect your career, but there will be a combined influence. This area relates to more than just your job; it represents your vocation, or your life path. It relates to the planet Mercury, winter, the times between 11pm and 1am and the element water. If you think of a river carving a path to the sea, this can be an analogy of how we carve out our lives from birth to death, learning and growing as we travel. So are you doing what you really want to do? Have you found your life path? If not, read on and discover how to make some alterations in that area (see also relating the five elements to the nine basic cures on pages 108-110).

Your health

The water element relates to your ears and the kidneys and you can treat them here. From the kidneys come your vitality. The kidneys store the energy passed on to us from our ancestors, they govern all the important functions of life from birth, growth, reproduction and sexuality to ageing. The amount of energy stored in the kidneys determines how long we will live. And the kidneys supply energy to all the other organs in the same way the front door supplies energy to all the other areas of your home. Water relates to your will-power so if you are persistent, alert, gentle but powerful and unafraid, this part of your house is strong. If you are fearful and find yourself 'running in circles' without getting anywhere, or if you are sexually overactive or stagnant, then this is another indication that we need to balance this area.

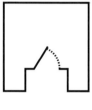

Missing area

When this area is missing from the house, the people who live there may find it harder to find their vocation and their general health will be weaker, making them more inclined to illness. The strength of our constitution comes from the kidneys, so it follows that if this area is missing then we are weaker.

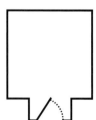

Extended area

If there is a small projection in this area, the occupants can acquire money and understand what to do with it. They can find their life path more easily. They will also tend to be interested in spiritual things and to have a strong and healthy constitution.

Area number 2: the relationship area

This area has the most feminine energy in the whole of the house. It relates to all one to one relationships; those with your spouse, your employer and/or employee and your friends. It is associated with the element earth, the warm, fertile, black earth that anything can grow in. It relates to the season of Indian summer, a time of plenty and the planet Saturn. The energy of the day between 1 and 3pm relates to the kind of energy found in this area. It is an area that is soft, stable, nurturing and should have a 'safe feeling'.

Your health   The organ that this area relates to is the spleen/stomach, which has the job of preparing the food, transporting it and feeding it to the other organs. It provides mental clarity and controls your thoughts and your short-term memory. The positive emotions of the spleen/stomach are duty and fairness (not having the stomach to do something wrong), nurturing, harmony, hospitality, steadiness and feeling centred. Its job is to balance. In the negative, the spleen represents complaining (being splenetic), having an excessive appetite and craving for more, feelings of insecurity and fear (yellow bellied), and needing lots of attention. To strengthen that part of your body, make changes in this area.

Missing area   If this area is missing it will be hard for a woman to be happy, and it will be very difficult to have satisfying relationships and find your life partner. The people who live here can tend to have stomach weakness and have difficulty nurturing themselves and others. The feminine energy is missing, so if there is a woman in the home, she can become more masculine.

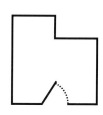

Extended area   If the area is extended, then the woman can become too dominant, weakening the man. This is not good for a woman, she naturally has less testosterone and it is more in keeping with her biological nature to be slightly softer, flexible and nurturing. So to be too dominant can damage her health.

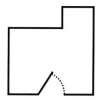

Area number 3: the ancestor area

This area relates to thunder, the planet Jupiter and early spring when all the new sprouts and buds are just bursting forth from the ground. It is associated with the element of wood and the time when the energy is strongest is between 5 and 8am. It relates to our ancestors, to whom we owe huge thanks, because if it weren't for them we wouldn't be here today. They gave us the gift of life. It also relates to people who are in a position of power over us, this might be the landlord, the leaseholder, the bank manager or, especially if you have your own business, your suppliers.

Your health   The area relates to the feet and the liver, so by making subtle changes in this area you can improve their health. The liver is the 'general' in charge of defending the body, it has the job of storing, filtering and making sure that blood flows to all parts of the body. It also transforms poisons into clean energy. The liver provides an energy that is akin to the morning sun. When the liver is in balance, you will be solicitous, full of spontaneous acts of kindness, cool headed, quick thinking, relaxed, clear minded, creative, progressive and willing to work as part of a team. This is indicative of the energy we find in the ancestor area. When the liver is out of balance, there is violence, irritability, a tendency to make big plans without being really clear about how you are going to achieve them, and being opportunistic, short tempered, loud, competitive and antagonistic. There is an expression that refers to people as being liverish and it means being full of anger.

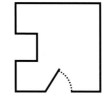

Missing area
If there is a missing area in this part of the bagua, residents will tend to feel less energetic and lack vitality, as the energy akin to spring is missing in the house. Family relationships may become tense and you may have difficulty starting new projects.

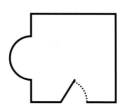

Extended area
If there is an extension in this area, it is regarded as lucky as there is a much greater chance of success in your vocation. And family relationships should be good, too, in a home of this shape.

Area number 4: the wealth area

This area relates to wind and communication, and late spring when all the trees are laden with blossom and the summer flowers are in bud. The area also relates to the time when the energy is similar to the hours between 8 and 11am. It relates to Jupiter, the element of wood, and this area also influences our finances and our luck and fortunate blessings. This includes all luck from winning at the race course to being blessed with good health and having a lovely family, to having pots of money.

Your health
The area relates to the muscles, hips, buttocks and especially the gall bladder, which has a gentler energy than the liver. It is the liver's sister organ so shares some of the qualities of the liver. Its function is to produce bile, which helps to digest fat and its qualities are lightness, fluidity and movement so it has the ability to move forwards easily. The negative is too much movement, instability, stagnancy interrupted by bursts of irritability and grumbling. You can treat that organ and the hips and muscles by making changes in this area of the home.

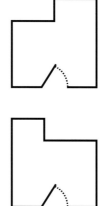

Missing area
If this area is missing, finances will be a struggle, good luck will always seem to bypass you and bad luck will be noticed instead. There can also be accidents, especially through being too impulsive.

Extended area
If this area is a little extended, it is very auspicious. The householders will experience successful business and generally be lucky in all things.

Area number 5: the Tai Chi area

The middle of the house is a yellow earth area and it is the vital centre. It relates to Saturn. The times when the energy is strongest are between 3 and 5am and 3 and 5pm. In China, this area would always be left open, there would be a courtyard in the centre. In the West we used to always have a chimney or a flue, also an open space. This area is concerned with your health and it unites all the other areas and establishes where they are. The Tai Chi contains everything and nothing, it is the yin and yang of the home.

Your health

By making changes in this area you help all aspects of health, especially the spleen, pancreas and stomach. As a combined unit, these organs have the ability to create or destroy, and they regulate all the other areas as everything has to pass through the centre. It provides the energy necessary to evaluate our lives and make necessary adjustment. If the area is blocked, there is no adjustment. It is an earth energy and water is the opposing force so we have to be careful of water in this area.

Missing area

It is not possible for this area to be missing, but it should be as bright, unblocked and empty as possible. It is not advisable to have a toilet or a bathroom at the heart of the house.

A house with an open courtyard in the centre means that the Tai Chi area is unblocked and promotes good health.

Extended area   It is also rather difficult for this area to be extended. If you have a courtyard in the centre of your house, make sure it is not more than a third of the total floor space of the indoor area.

Area number 6: the benefactors area

This area belongs to the metal element and it relates to steel, crystal and diamonds. It relates to friends who are angels and will support you during times of need, it also relates to charity and travel. It is the most masculine part of the house. It relates to autumn when all the leaves have gone and all the crops have been gathered and it is a time of contraction and discipline because now the crops have been gathered they must last until the next season. The energy in this area relates most to the time between 9 and 11pm.

Your health   By making changes in this area you can help the large intestine, the great eliminator. This area is often associated with philanthropy and charity. When in balance, the qualities are clarity, generosity, fairness, purity, respect, honour and courage. The negatives are depression, attachment, dishonesty, stinginess, rigidity and not being able to forgive. The head is also treated in this area, so if you are inclined to headaches or any mental stress, you may need to make some subtle changes here.

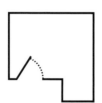

Missing area   If this area is missing then it is hard for a man to be happy and he will tend to spend more time outside the house than is necessary. He will tend not to come home for supper, he will probably work later in the office than necessary, and he may find it difficult to get on with his employers. He can also suffer from ill health and be weak in his own house.

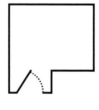

Extended area   When there is a projection in this area, people who live here will become more charitable and supportive of people who have less than they have. You can also expect to travel more and not only expect to have lots of friends or angels around you, you will also tend to be seen as a great friend to others.

Area number 7: the children area

The children area relates to Venus and gold (its element is metal), and it is known as the creative, the lake, or joy in the I Ching. It doesn't just relate to children but also to your hobbies and pet projects, that kit car in the garage – your 'baby', the things you get excited about. The area relates to joy and pleasure and early autumn, when the leaves are brilliant

colours, laden with fruits and there is gluttony and plenty. The time that relates most to this area is between 5 and 8pm.

A round house has good feng shui because it does not have as many corners where stagnant energy can collect.

Your health

The organ that can be treated in this area is the lung. The lung controls the skin, which is known as the third lung, and its job is to mix chi from the air with energy from food. It is linked with expression, taking in and breathing out. In balance, the qualities stored in the lungs are intuition, crisp, cool, mental clarity, a quick mind, determination, courage and being able to forgive and understand. The negative qualities are depression, grief, jealousy, unreliability, not being able to forgive, pettiness and resentment. The mouth opens into this area, so if you are a singer or a teacher you may need to pay special emphasis to this sector in your home.

Missing area

If the area is missing then there will be little joy, residents will not have any hobbies and it can be difficult to conceive children. It will be hard to spend money on any pleasurable activity and it will tend to be spent in different ways, like having to lend it to a family in need or to repair the house.

Extended area

When this area is extended, the people who live here will have more pleasure and joy in their lives, they will be sociable, enjoy good intuition and happiness. It will be easier to conceive children and you can expect to maintain good relationships with them. This is a very good place to have an extension.

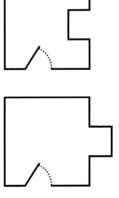

27

Area number 8: the knowledge area

This is a white earth area and it relates to the 'earth' of porcelain. It is like a mountain with a hard veneer and softness deep inside, such that it symbolises a container. The knowledge area relates to the hours between 1 and 4am, the time of stillness before dawn has begun, and the time when revolution and change are carefully plotted. It is an area where you can realise what you want and what is happening in your life. This particular area also relates to inner knowledge, and the chi here is still, and a little bit dangerous: this is the area that spirits come in through.

Your health
Be careful how and where you put water in this area. The knowledge area relates to the pancreas, the deepest organ in the body, and the most yang of all the organs. To keep this area healthy, happy and strong it needs to be warm and bright so choose your decorating colours carefully. The knowledge area also relates to your hands so if you have arthritis in your hands, or you are a painter or a sculptor, you may want to place some cures here such as a crystal or something pink (as outlined in the nine basic cures on pages 108-25).

The fame area (see area number 9) of this house is weak, so it will be harder to gain promotion.

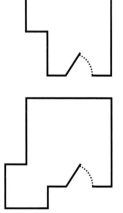

Missing area
If the area is missing, people living here will tend not to be very interested in learning anything new or reading books. They will tend to be inflexible in their views and it can be more difficult for a couple to conceive a child while living in this house.

Extended area
If the area is extended, it can lead to the occupants becoming more selfish, but they will have enquiring minds and always be interested in learning something new.

Area number 9: the fame area

This area relates to fame and promotion and it has an influence upon your career and upon enlightenment. It relates to Mars and the element is fire. The season is summer when everything is in blossom and the days are beautiful and sunny. The time the energy in this area relates to most specifically is between 11am and 1pm. This area relates to fame not just from the perspective of being a star but also to the fire of illumination from within. Many people become famous and then leave behind the glitter and limelight and find they want to follow a much quieter dream and they start to know themselves better. Enlightened masters often abandon publicity and seek a more private life.

Your health
The parts of your body associated with this area are the heart and small intestine and you can strengthen them by placing cures here. The heart is the home of the spirit, and the spirit has the best energies from all the other organs. These are the qualities of love, kindness, joy, gentleness, courage and fairness, warmth, refinement, respect, brightness and spirituality. The fire energy is expansive and energetic, it feeds inspiration, the power of genius. There are many expressions relating to the heart from heart warming, coming from the heart, and hearty, to hard hearted or heartless. In the negative, there is cruelty, coldness, selfishness, vanity and one who is inconsiderate. The eyes open into this area, so if you are suffering from any complaints of the eye you can place a cure here.

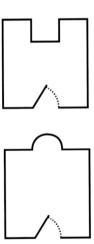

Missing area
When this area is missing it is harder to get promotion, and the people living there tend to care too much about what people think.

Extended area
When the area is extended you will tend to be well known in the community, neighbours will know your name and your business and you will be well liked. It is easier to become famous.

Using the bagua template on your car

You can apply feng shui to your car. The mouth of chi is where the engine of the car is, so if the engine is in the rear of the car then lay the bagua template over the car so that the relationship area is in the front right-hand side seat, and the wealth area is in the left. If your engine is in the front of the car, lay the bagua template with the career area over the bonnet, the relationship area over the right-hand passenger seat, and the wealth area over the left seat. If you subsequently lose a hub cap, or you or somebody else should dent or scratch the car, wherever the damage is will have an impact upon that facet of your life.

Applying feng shui

The entrance to your world

The 'mouth of chi' is usually your front door, or the door where the postman comes to deliver the mail. It is the one that people automatically come to when they are visiting your house for the first time. This door relates to your life path, your vocation. It is the most important door in the house and is known as the 'mouth of chi' because most of the energy in your home comes in here, you walk it in each time you enter. Chi can come through walls, and a percentage comes in through the windows, but most comes through the main entrance. Try to get into the habit of changing your footwear when you go into the house. Your shoes can absorb a lot of energy that would be better kept outside.

What does your front door look like? Go and have a good look now. Is it chipped with peeling paint, does it have tarnished door furniture and a broken bell? If it is, then life can seem like a constant battle and there will probably be lots of quarrels in your life and you may have to fight to reach your goals. Likewise, the front door relates to your relationship

Fountains are natural ionisers and they also attract wild life into the garden. The shutter in front of the door counteracts the amount of glass in the door itself.

with the outside world. If it is sticking, your life will probably be full of irritations that slow down your progress.

If the door cannot open fully, because lots of coats and shoes have accumulated near the door, or maybe a radiator has been inappropriately positioned, then the house will only receive a percentage of the energy it should be getting. Therefore, few opportunities come in and over time you can become introverted. So, if your door is blocked, go and clear it right away.

Achieving a front door with good feng shui

● When you open your front door you should walk into the main part of the room, not into the wall. When you have the door open to its widest extent it should be parallel to the wall.

● Don't let your door furniture become tarnished or blemished; instead it should always be bright and gleaming to help keep money flowing in. You can paint chrome and brass with varnish so you do not have to spend every Sunday polishing!

● If you have a round, shiny door knob which is highly polished it can deflect negative energy.

● There should always be a step into your house. Roads are regarded as rivers and if you are below the level of the river you are inviting danger.

● The front door should be the same size or slightly larger than all the others. It should also be in the middle of the wall and open inwardly so that chi gets channelled into the house rather that out of it.

● If your front door consists of half or more glass, energy will tend to come and go too freely which means you have less control over all aspects of your life and your health will be more delicate. This is exacerbated if your stairs are facing the front

Evergreen plants in round containers conduct healthy chi into the house. The step up to the front door and shiny door furniture also make this an auspicious entrance.

door. If your door has a small pane of glass in it, put in blue and yellow stained glass or hang a small spherical faceted crystal in the window. If there is too large an area of glass, it is best to change the door for a completely solid one.

● Windows positioned on either side of the front door can make it difficult for you to be in control of your life. Unpredictable things will keep happening, putting you off balance. So close them up or screen them with curtains or round-leafed plants on the window sills.

● Mechanical bells vibrate in such a way that they cleanse the atmosphere when they are chimed. This kind of door bell is preferable to an electric bell, but make sure you like the sound.

● Hang wind chimes in the area between the front door and the stairs if your stairs face the front door or if your front door is lined up with the back door. They slow down energy by creating a little obstacle high up which reduces the speed of the flow and prevent things from happening beyond your control.

● People who live in a grey, damp climate like Northern Europe can benefit from having the influence of some fire energy, so it is auspicious to add a splash of red or yellow on or near your front door, perhaps in the shape of coloured pot planters.

● The number or name of your house should be hung at an upward slant to lift the chi energy associated with your house.

These noble beasts belong to the earth element and have been situated to protect the house by facing away from the front door.

What can you tell from the way your front door is facing?

South-facing
The Chinese place so much importance on this direction that they always place it at the top of their compasses, while the rest of us put north there. The energy coming into the south-facing house is the most conducive to life. It tends to be bright, warm and sunny, and it is represented by summer. It is an energy that is happy and active. A front door that is facing in this direction has many happy associations such as fame, fortune, celebration and happiness. If a shop or business faces this direction it is likely to be prosperous. The best colour to paint a front door facing this direction is green or red or else leave it as a natural wood finish.

Southwest-facing
A southwest-facing front door can be good for relationships but partly because it is influenced by being the door opposite the unfavourable northeast. It can, however, bring more sickness into the house so you need to hang up a wind chime above the front door to dispel this influence (see the fourth cure, page 114). The door can be painted red or yellow and be finished with well polished, shiny metal door furniture.

West-facing
A front door facing in this direction means that the energy in your home will tend to be tranquil and peaceful. During the timespan of 1984-2003 lots of money, pleasure and opportunity can come in making this is the most auspicious orientation for your front door during this particular twenty-year cycle. The best colours for this door are yellow, orange, burgundy, white or metallic.

Northwest-facing
The energy coming in through a door that faces northwest is especially good for the male members of the family. The occupants will be work-orientated and it should be easy for them to gain support from people in positions of power. If your door faces this direction you will probably travel a lot, though it can be hard to hold onto your finances. Doors facing in this direction should be painted white, yellow, orange, terracotta or burgundy with chrome or brass door furniture.

North-facing
If your front door is orientated to the north, the energy coming into the home is cold, grey, gloomy and not conducive to life. It is not generally a recommended direction, because it is associated with the bleakness of winter and death. The animals that were chosen to symbolize the north are the tortoise or the deer (see the seventh cure, page 118) because they represent longevity, balancing the association with death.

If your door faces north you can take heart because it relates to water, and water is associated with money so this is an orientation where money can flow in. If you have such a door, good colours to paint it are blue, black or white with gold door furniture, and locate pictures on or above the door. Alternatively, position statues of tortoises or deer on either side of the door outside and facing away from the house.

Northeast-facing
If the door is orientated to the northeast, the household can be more academic as the energy coming from this direction relates to knowledge and learning. But, this is traditionally known as the door that spirits come in through and is not recommended, especially as many of us don't remember our ancestors at all. Hang up a bagua mirror (see the first cure, page 111) above the front door so that it shines into the street and paint the door red, yellow or an earth colour.

East-facing
If your front door is facing east, your house will receive the energy of the rising sun, which is associated with growth, new enterprises, good family life and strong health. A dragon-shaped door knob would be fortuitous and the door should be painted blue, black, green or have a natural wood finish.

Southeast-facing
Many of the directions are related to finances, but the southeast-facing front door is associated most strongly with wealth. The energy in your home is going to be active as you have the late morning energy coming into the house. The door should be painted blue or black with brass door furniture or if you want painted door furniture, paint it black, blue or green and paint the front door green, purple or a natural wood finish.

What's in a number

Oriental people have a great respect for numbers. You will often find streets that are numbered 8, 18, 78 and 88 because town planners and powerful property developers have discovered that everybody wants to live in a house that has an auspicious eight in it.

The Chinese use an interesting technique for translating house names into numbers. The number of strokes of the pen you make to write the letter is the number of the letter, so in this way it is entirely personal to you and your writing. Once you have established the numbers for all the letters of the word, add them up to give you the overall number. So, for example:

FENG SHUI COMPANY
2 2 3 2 + 1 3 2 1 + 1 1 4 2 3 3 2 = 32

BALLARD HOUSE
2 3 2 2 3 2 2 + 3 1 1 1 2 = 24

Auspicious Chinese numbers are:

3, 5, 6, 8, 11, 13, 15, 16, 17, 18, 21, 23, 24, 25, 29, 31, 32, 33, 35, 37, 39, 48, 52, 63, 73, 75, 77, 78, 80, 81, 83, 84, 87, 8, 89, 90, 91, 92, 97, 98, 99, 100

The vibration received from your house number

1 A house that is number 1, or reduces down to number 1, will be a one house. One will have the influence of helping you to really develop as an individual, and find your life path. It is a house of independence and you will tend to learn from your experiences rather than listening to other people. It is difficult to live in harmony with other people in this home and there will be a tendency to isolate yourself. It also indicates prosperity in small amounts.

2 This number can bring sickness which can be rectified quite simply by having your house number made out of metal, or mounting it on a metal plaque, and hanging a wind chime above the front door. It is a good house number for a couple because it is easy to live in harmony with someone. It is possible to tune into other people while living in this house, so your empathy and compassion will be strengthened. You can become a little too dependent, though, and take on too many responsibilities. People who live in this house tend to be very rational thinkers.

3 This number resonates with fun and laughter. It will be a social house of expansion and good communication where things can happen very quickly. It can be a quarrelsome house though, but the quarrels won't last long. Number 3 is the first spiritual number so it denotes a certain sensitivity and intuition. You need to be a bit careful of finances because there can be a tendency to be over-confident and push forward too impulsively.

4 The word for four sounds phonetically exactly like the Chinese word for death so it is regarded with some suspicion and avoided in the Orient. If you imagine giving your address to someone in Chinese and you lived at number four, you would be saying 'I live at Death the High Street', or 'Death Wood Lane'. Try saying your own address with death as a prefix and you will get a sense of how the Chinese feel. It is advisable to avoid houses with this number if you go to live in the East because this house will have a psychological cloud over it. But in feng shui, four is considered as auspicious in certain situations. The four vibration represents logic, discipline, and hard work, and it will be a stable house. It is very grounded and relates to hard, steady work and a good, steady financial income.

5 A house which is number 5 is a powerful house. It is a house where the occupants tend to always be at the centre of things. It is also a house of balance and control; the energy can be very creative and when out of balance, destructive. There can also be a tendency towards arrogance. A number 5 house is a difficult one to study in because there is too much activity but if living in this house you can reach incredible achievements. It is the second spiritually

The Western technique

Every letter is given a number, as shown in the chart to the right. The letters of your address can be given numbers which are then added up to give a total. If you have a house number, use that alone and find out more about your home's vibration from the chart below. Otherwise, work out your number, using either your house name or company name. If the total has more than one digit in it, these numbers are then added together, and again if necessary, until you are left with only one number. Then consult the chart below.

Number assignations

a	b	c	d	e	f	g	h	i
j	k	l	m	n	o	p	q	r
s	t	u	v	w	x	y	z	
1	2	3	4	5	6	7	8	9

So, for the Feng Shui Company, the numbers are:

FENG   SHUI   COMPANY
6 5 5 7 + 1 8 3 9 + 3 6 4 7 1 5 7
= 90 = 9

numbered house and so is thought of as a karmic house where everything and anything can happen.

6 Number 6 has a practical vibration and is indicative of financial good fortune in medium measures. The people who live here will tend to be philanthropic and socially minded and it is a good house in which to bring up a family. In this house you may find that you have to be a bit careful with your money because it can have the vibration of having a wealthy childhood and youth but beginning to struggle as you reach middle age and possibly difficulties by the time you get to old age. So, if you live in a house that is number 6 put some money aside for a rainy day.

7 Living in a house that has a seven vibration means it has a spiritual vibration and for the 20-year cycle covering 1984 to 2003, it is the most auspicious number to live at as seven is the reigning number. After 2003, do like the Chinese and change the number to eight! (So if your street numbers run from 1 to 30, change your house number to 38 or 88 or even 8a.) In another context, seven makes you especially sensitive to the meaning of our existence, the metaphysical aspects of life. It is a mystical number that represents wisdom. A seven house is difficult to share with other people, but it is a good house to study in and also to make money at the same time as learning about the spirit world – but only until 2003, then the material side will seem to be lacking.

8 The vibration of an eight house exerts powerful influences on wealth. It is an intrinsically lucky number representing great good fortune in the present and the future. The number is balanced and harmonious. You can acquire good judgement and become a good business person. You can have lots of friends, gain self-knowledge, self-power, honours and promotion. In this house, you can reach spiritual, physical and mental heights. The danger is that you can become too materialistic and the money can create problems unless you make sure you look after the welfare of others with some of your wealth.

9 When you live in a house that is number nine, you are living under the influence of the intellect and it is regarded as an auspicious number. It signifies that the people who live there will be clever, ambitious and self-assured. They will also possess a degree of authority. Living in this house can help you to achieve recognition and develop your career fast.

● If your house number has a zero in it, it brings an added influence of power to the ordinary number and also adds a spiritual dimension to the numbers.

● House numbers that are in double figures like 31 have the vibration of each of these numbers, but crowning them is the 4 (3+1 = 4). If you live at number 56, 5+6=11=2, the crowning number is the 2, but 5 and 6 and 1 also have a significant, if softer, influence.

The front garden

If you have a path that leads up to your front door, it should ideally meander like a lazy river across the front garden and it should be wider at the street and narrower at the front door and not be made of crazy paving. If it is a straight path all of one width, it sends poison arrows to the house by conducting energy too fast which can cause accidents and things to happen beyond your control. If the pathway is narrower at the street than the front door it makes it difficult for you to find employment – this has a more negative influence upon the male members of the family than the female.

If the path is shaped like a T-junction at the front door so that, say, you have the choice of going to the garage or the garden immediately you step out of the house, it can make you indecisive, and cause you to go round in little circles not achieving very much. To make the decision easier to make, lay out paths so that they fork from the front door rather than the rigid T-junction. The ideal layout is a main path leading to the street with a tributary forking off, say, to the garage.

Driveways should also be wider at the street and narrower nearer the house and, of course, meandering in gentle curves. Other auspicious shapes for drives are horse-shoe shaped (having a separate entrance and exit) or having a circular island in the centre.

The top of a garden gate should curve up at a happy angle and preferably be made of metal. Make sure it opens smoothly and silently – it if squeaks it can damage your liver.

Happy or sad: what's in a name?

If your house has a name, make sure it's a happy one. I once went to Australia and visited a beach called the Cape of Despair. During the journey there we couldn't help feeling a bit flat about the prospect of going to a place with such a name. When we got there, it was beautiful but everybody was still quiet. By comparison, my friend Miranda has a summer house called Faraway Cottage. When she invites me there for the weekend, all through the week I think to myself, 'I'm off to Faraway Cottage' – it sounds so romantic and adventurous and it lifts my spirits before I've even arrived. It is always an enjoyable journey with lots of bright chatter and as soon as we arrive, no matter how late

or what the weather is like, we always run straight down to the sea.

Your house takes on the energy of its name. Some time ago I gave a consultation to a young woman who lived in a big, rather neglected, house. Among the recommendations I suggested she gave the house a name. Recently she rang me to say she had finally thought of the right name: 'Avro', which means in Greek a warm and welcoming light. From that time on she felt she was going home to a warm and welcoming light and the house took on a whole new character. So do remember this when thinking of a name and call your house something happy.

It is important that you keep the path leading to your front door clutter free so that energy isn't restricted; it is also preferable to have a winding path that is wider at the street end than at the house. Further ways to improve the vibrations in a front garden are given overleaf.

Position door numbers so that they rise upwards to lift the chi.

If you have some glass in your front door, make sure it is stained yellow and blue.

Position an evergreen plant in a round container on each side of the front door.

Keep all flower beds curved.

Keep all brass door furniture shiny and clean – a tarnished entrance is a blocked entrance.

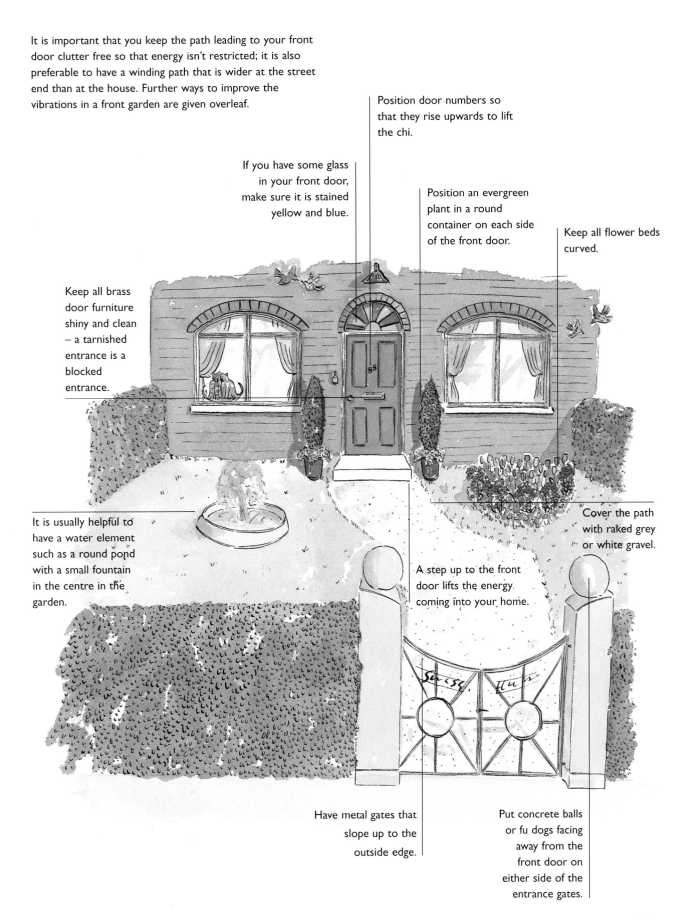

It is usually helpful to have a water element such as a round pond with a small fountain in the centre in the garden.

Cover the path with raked grey or white gravel.

A step up to the front door lifts the energy coming into your home.

Have metal gates that slope up to the outside edge.

Put concrete balls or fu dogs facing away from the front door on either side of the entrance gates.

39

It is always good to have a meandering path leading up to your front door. It is even better if it is narrower at the door end than the entrance.

Achieving good feng shui in a front garden

● If, when you leave your home, you have to battle past a collection of bins, overgrown plants and jumble you will have limited opportunity coming into your life. So keep the entrance nice and clear.

● The area outside your front door should be brightly lit but make sure the outside light does not dazzle motorists or pedestrians.

● If you have a tree or a lamp post directly opposite the front door, you need to hang a convex mirror (see the first cure, page 111) on the lintel to combat the negative influence.

● If you have a manhole on the path directly in front of the front door, put a mat over it. If it is slightly to the right or left, put a planter on top of it.

● The drains relate to your finances and your intestines so just make sure they are not blocked. If you live in a tropical country and if your house faces north, south, east or west, the water should be flowing from left to right. If your front door is facing northeast, northwest, southeast or southwest, the water from the drains should be flowing from right to left.

● I often recommend people lay raked grey or white gravel at the front of their houses because it represents the sea which is beneficial in this area, and it is also low maintenance.

● It is usually very auspicious to have water at the front of the house as it can bring more opportunity into your life.

● Plants (see the eighth cure, page 121) are wonderful producers of healthy chi and keeping a round planter on either side of your front door (the larger one to the east or the north depending which way your house is facing) with something evergreen and something flowering in them (during the blossoming months) will conduct healthy chi into the house.

● It is not a good idea to park your car right up by the front door. We think of cars as tigers, they move too fast and put a pressure on the house (see overleaf).

● You should place either heavy boulders, brick gate posts, concrete balls, Fu dogs or their equivalent on either side of the entrance to your driveway, especially if your drive slopes away from the house as the energy is falling away. Fu dogs are lion dogs and they look quite ferocious. Their job is twofold: not only do they prevent energy from leaking out of the house, but they also deter burglars on a psychological level. The fu dogs give the feeling that the house is well guarded.

● Fu dogs should always be sited in pairs otherwise it is unlucky. If you purchase your fu dogs from an antique shop, be sure to find out where they came from: if they used to belong to a temple or similar they can be filled with an energy that you may not be able to control, in which case it is better to buy them new. In the West, we have the equivalent in the shape of lions or griffins with shields, and you can use these just as effectively.

● If you put lights on pillars on either side of the entrance to your drive it will bring more energy into your home.

Inside the house

The relationship of the front and back doors to each other can affect the feng shui in your home. If your front door is lined up with the back door, it means things will happen in your life that you can't control, and it means that money will come in and go rushing out. It creates a wind tunnel effect which upsets our balance, affecting the nervous system and so performance at work and decision-making capabilities.

The problem is compounded if you have front or back doors with any glass in them (see page 33-4). If you have this unfortunate situation, make both doors solid and if there is space, place an item of furniture like a console against one side of the wall. This will encourage people to walk in a meandering way and slow down the energy. You can also hang a bead curtain between the doors or a small silver mayan ball (see the first cure, page 111) from red ribbon in the window of the back door to reflect the energy. But the best solution is to close up the back door and relocate it somewhere else.

A couple I know had been living very happily in a house and in a fit of DIY enthusiasm they decided to install a glass door opposite the front door, which also had a large proportion of glass. Within

A staircase that doesn't lead straight down to the front door is the best orientation; this prevents the house's energy from draining out through the door.

The lovely warm earth colours on this front door are very welcoming as it opens wide into the knowledge area.

a week the gentleman of the household was made redundant, which meant the couple might lose their house because they would have difficulty with the mortgage payments. As they both lived in a rural area and were in their fifties, things were looking fairly bleak. They closed up the back door and shortly afterwards, the gentleman's employers telephoned and offered to extend his contract by another five years, which meant the house was safe.

The function of your hallway is to lead you from one room to the next and to create separate rooms. Your hall can be compared to the central river that feeds all the little tributaries. If there is a blockage, the little tributaries can dry up. Carrying the analogy further: if your hall is blocked and cluttered, all the other areas of your life are going to suffer. As if that isn't enough, if the hallway is very blocked it can make you depressed, influence your health and worst of all, make you stuck so you can't change your situation easily. Don't let it happen.

Achieving good feng shui in a hallway

● The area inside your front door is called the ming tang, or bright spot. If the area is dark and dingy it will be difficult to find your life path. So make sure you have a bright light in the hall, and that it is light, fresh and welcoming. It should be uncluttered with enough space to move freely from one room to another.

● Corridors should not be long and narrow as narrow corridors squeeze chi and can turn it from beneficial to unstable energy.

● Spiral staircases can damage your health, especially if they are in the middle of the house. Energy that is forced to twist and funnel up becomes destructive (it's interesting how often spiral staircases are featured in horror films). A spiral staircase must twist round on top of itself at least once to qualify as a spiral.

- Stairs should not be directly in front of the front door as your energy will then drain out of the door. Ideally, they should be wide, curving and shallow. This helps energy to move gently.

- The house should be more or less the same temperature throughout or it can create arguments and health problems.

- The electrical system relates to your nervous system so if you have lots of overloaded plugs and exposed wires they can 'stress' your nervous system.

- The windows relate to your eyes, so keep them sparkling clean. Replace any cracked glass with fresh panes – you want to see the world as it really is.

- Bagua mirrors (see the first cure, page 111) draw in positive energy and deflect all sorts of negative energy. If a front door is suffering from a threatening influence, a mirror can be hung on it, above it or on either side shining towards the influence.

- You might hang a bagua mirror (see the first cure, page 111) in a window or above your front door so that the mirrored part shines out to deflect a tall block of flats opposite (if you find all the windows a little threatening). If you have a church, hospital, police station, mental asylum, underground railway or such-like near your house, then use a bagua mirror to deflect the negative sha.

- You might hang a bagua mirror (see the first cure, page 111) above the front door if you were using your home as a business with lots of clients visiting who are poorly, if you are in a healing profession, say. It is important even if you just have a few people who you don't know very well, like a secretary, a nanny or an assistant, visiting your home. It will have the effect of warding off any people who mean you or your family harm in any way.

Garages or workshops

Ideally, garages should be separate from the house because cars should be parked some distance away. In feng shui we think of cars as tigers, when you switch the lights on for the first time they glow orange for a second – like a tiger's eyes. They also move too fast and funnel malignant chi in a dangerous way, and they threaten the residents in the house. If your garage is attached to the house, it should not have any part of the house behind it or the car will put pressure on the residents.

The garage should be north-facing to keep the tiger's energy quiet and separate from the house. If you can get to your garage from the house and it has part of the house behind it and some above it then turn the garage into an extra room. If this isn't possible, try to make the room behind the garage into a room that is used only occasionally, like a laundry room or store room. If you don't do this, accidents can befall the occupants.

Sitting rooms

The sitting room relates to the side of you that you show to the outside world. It is a place to show off to your friends, or to gather in, where you can relax and enjoy yourself after a hard day's work. It therefore doesn't need to be functional like a kitchen should be, it just needs to be warm, comfortable, welcoming and recreational.

As already discovered, rule number one for any room in your house is no clutter (see pages 14-17). If your sitting room is full of magazines, books, plants, games, knitting and all sorts of things, it makes it difficult for you to relax. More than any other room, this one should feel warm and cosy so you can put up your feet after the chores of the day are over. If something keeps catching your eye, like that empty cup of coffee, you can't settle down because you know it ought to be in the kitchen.

Perhaps the most important thing in this room in the twentieth century is the television set. This object has a powerful energy that sends out EMF signals for up to three days after it has been switched off. This means that you are drawn to the television even when it is switched off. When it is on, it can be almost hypnotic because it functions in the spectrum of the alpha brain wave range which automatically forces us into a relaxed, hypnotic state. Have you ever witnessed your children, your partner or even yourself absolutely transfixed to the screen?

A simple, if rather crude, way to test the area surrounding an electrical appliance is to tune an AM radio between stations, turn the volume up and waves over a certain level, about one milligausse, can be heard as static. With the AM radio you can approximately detect where high field emitters are in your area, and when you are within too close a range of the electrical appliances in your home.

The beaded curtain in this sitting room has been cleverly hung to create a smaller, cosier sitting space within the larger area.

In order to balance the television energy it should be kept in a built-in cupboard and you should shut the cupboard doors occasionally so that you can use this room to play games in or just talk without being distracted by the television. If you have something bright and eye-catching like a fish tank near the television, it will draw some of the energy away from the television.

When you live in a large house with several rooms for gathering, like a playroom, a drawing room, a TV room or a morning room, separation can all too easily occur. To counterbalance this, try to encourage everyone to use one family room during certain hours. It can become a little chaotic, but it keeps the family unit strong. Dare I suggest that you could try just having one television in the house?

There are two sitting areas in this room: one for chatting in with the chairs grouped around a coffee table and log fire, and the other for watching television. The large plants freshen the atmosphere.

45

If you have the space, it is best to arrange the furniture in your sitting room in two separate areas: one for chatting in with the chairs arranged in a friendly circle, and the other for watching television. The best colours for painting a sitting room are yellow, purple, pink or peach – anything warm and inviting. Further ways to improve the vibrations in a sitting room are given overleaf.

Hang curtains on the windows rather than blinds as these are softer.

Large plants in the sitting room are invaluable for soaking up electric vibrations from the television set.

Install a real flame fire and light it every night to enhance the friendly atmosphere of the sitting room.

A fish tank or light should be positioned in the corner of the room to bring in peace.

If you must have a television in your sitting room, position it in a cupboard so that you can close the doors on it once you have finished watching it.

Wood is the best material for a coffee table, and a round or oval shape has a more gathering influence.

Keep all shelving as low-level as possible to prevent the feeling that they will come toppling down on you.

Position the chairs so that they face the door rather than have their backs to it. If there is a large space behind a chair, put a screen or bookshelf there to prevent feelings of vulnerability.

Achieving good feng shui in a sitting room

● The sitting room is busiest during the evening when it is often cold so the colours need to have warmth in them, especially if the room faces the northeast or north. So the best colours for the room are the ones with a warm and gathering influence like harvest colours, yellows, highlights of red or magenta, purple, pink, peach, orange or cream. If you decide to use a lot of grey or blue, for example, you will need to balance it with yellow to maintain the gathering effect.

● There is nothing that can compete with the auspicious and gathering influence of a log fire or a real flame fire. If you can, use it every night, it will have a beneficial influence on your sitting room.

● If your sitting room is big enough, divide it into two areas. One for television viewing with the chairs arranged around it, and another area for chatting, with the seats arranged around a coffee table. When you are sitting in the 'chatting area', light a candle (see the third cure, page 113) on the coffee table and it will keep everybody's attention drawn around the table.

● Any coffee table in your sitting room should be made from wood and be round or oval because of the gathering influence. If you have a rectangular coffee table it can act as a barrier, keeping people apart from you. A glass surface makes a jarring sound when things are put on it, so avoid this material.

This sofa is lined up too directly with the entrance and will tend to draw people out of the room. Another sofa or screen placed opposite would counteract the influence.

- It is important that you have at least one, big, plant to absorb electrical pollution and freshen the atmosphere.

- Position the chairs and sofas so that you have a view of the door. This is obviously not always possible, so you can position a screen, dresser, bookcase or similar behind exposed seats to make the person feel more secure.

- The power seat of the room is the one with the best view of the door and window, and this seat should be occupied by an adult or parent. If you let a child sit here, he or she can become disobedient and rebellious.

- Indoor waterfalls combined with a light have a favourable influence in this room. The water functions like a natural ioniser and the light prevents it from having a dispersing influence. It is best situated in the corner of the room to the far left as you are standing facing in to the entrance of the room.

- If you have a chandelier it will draw in people and help the conversation to sparkle. You may need some task lighting as well if you read or sew in this room.

- The careful orientation of mirrors can make the room appear more spacious and sunnier, especially if you can reflect the garden or water in to the house.

- Generally it is good to hang pictures of groups of people playing cards or sitting around a fire laughing and chatting to promote that sort of influence in the room.

- Hanging a spherical faceted crystal will keep sunshine energy dancing around the room.

- Keep all shelving as low-level as possible to prevent the feeling that everything is tumbling down on you.

- Curtains are preferable in the sitting room to any other form of window treatment as they create by the far the softest atmosphere.

- If you have a sha outside your house like a block of flats with many windows, the mayan ball (see the first cure, page 111) can deflect it. They are not as strong as a bagua mirror but they don't look as oriental. They should be hung from a length of red ribbon clearly visible from outside, so if you have net curtains it will need to be hung between the net and the glass. Make sure it is not obscured by any part of the window frame.

Kitchens

The kitchen is often regarded as the heart of the house and, as such, is one of the most important rooms. It should be a warm, cosy place with wonderful smells. It has a strong influence on our finances and on our liver, so if the kitchen is a mess, tempers may fray more easily, wherever it is located.

As usual, you must always think about the clutter in your kitchen. Do you really need two kettles in the kitchen? Will you ever use those spices you brought back from Grenada, and those pickled quails eggs that have been sitting in your cupboard for years? Wouldn't all those greasy cookery books that you only use occasionally be better in the study? If the

The rounded edges on the cupboards and work surfaces make this kitchen a safe and friendly space.

children do their homework on the kitchen table and leave it out, it's distracting. If you have too much going on in your kitchen, you can lose clarity, feel overwhelmed and your finances will not be so strong. This is not the place to do anything except cook and chat. The energy should be fresh and clean, gathering and bright. The atmosphere should be one of warmth, bustle, cleanliness, freshness and action.

Achieving good feng shui in a kitchen

● Kitchens should have an energy that is clean, fresh, gathering and bright. It is better to have mainly cupboards with few or no shelves. Keep all your surfaces clear.

The best place to situate the hob is on an island in the centre of the kitchen so that the chef has a clear view of everything that is happening in the rest of the room.

51

The best colours for painting a kitchen are white and yellow with only a small amount of black or dark blue. The most important item in the kitchen is the hob and this is best situated on an island towards the centre of the room in such a place that the chef can see the rest of the room while cooking. Further ways to improve the vibrations in a kitchen are given on the previous page and overleaf.

Have a stainless steel sink and preferably position it in front of the window.

Keep all knives out of sight.

Keep all edges to worktops and tables rounded and preferably made of wood.

Put a reflective material around the hob to contain the fire's energy.

Hang a crystal in the window if the view outside is ugly – this will reflect the energy away from the kitchen.

Do not position the fridge or sink opposite or next to the hob - such mixing of fire and water is inauspicious.

Keep all your crockery matching.

Kitchens should be painted in glossy, durable and easily cleanable paint. The flooring should be wood, linoleum or tiles; avoid carpet. The colour depends slightly upon where the kitchen falls in the bagua, but generally auspicious colours are white, yellow and a small amount of black or dark blue.

All worktops and units should have rounded corners to stop you from damaging yourself and to prevent your money from slipping off the edge.

If you have more than one door, especially if the doors are lined up so that they are opposite each other, the kitchen will become a corridor with too much activity passing through. This is disturbing for the chef, so aim for a kitchen with only one door. The kitchen will then be a tranquil, peaceful place where the cook can be relaxed and calm.

A clean and unblocked sink keeps your finances flowing, even more so if the sink is made from stainless steel as this is a symbol of prosperity.

I have noticed that when someone has a matching crockery service it creates an atmosphere of harmony and freshness that mismatched china can never achieve.

Knives send out cutting chi and they create arguments so always keep them out of sight, preferably in a kitchen drawer or in a block.

Bins should always have a lid on them. And try and get into the habit of emptying them every day.

The hob and the cooker are the most important appliances, and they should always be real flame. The best place to site your hob is to inset it onto an island in the centre of the kitchen to encourage the room to become the heart of the house, just as it should be. The hob should also have a surround, about 7.5-10 cm (3-4 in) high, of highly reflective metal on the side near the flames. This doubles the energy of the burners. The other side of the surround is best served by being made of wood to protect the fingers of the people who will tend to sit opposite you and help when you are cooking. There should not be enough space for someone to walk behind the cook when dishes are being created. If you cannot site your hob on an island, at least avoid aligning it with the kitchen door, especially if it is the main entrance into the kitchen. Do not position it so that it is against a window or your finances will tend to evaporate! If your cooker is against a wall, fix either a mirror or a sheet of shiny stainless steel behind the hob. This will reflect the burners, which doubles your finances, and the cook can see what is going on behind, making for a much more contented chef. To prevent stagnation in any area of your life, rotate the burners so that you use a different burner each time you cook. It is regarded as highly unlucky to site a cooker (fire element) next to or opposite a fridge, dishwasher, washing machine or sink, as these are water elements and the two energies do not mix harmoniously and it can create quarrels. So make sure that they are not directly opposite each other and that there is at least a 500 mm (20 in) width and length of surface between each element.

- The cooker is best situated on an east, southeasterly, or southwesterly wall. The least auspicious is the north which can create conflict, or the south which can create fires in the house.

- The second most important item in the kitchen is the fridge (the holder of the goodies) and the best colour for the fridge is white, silver, blue, green or panelled in wood.

- The worst place to locate the fridge is on the south, southwest or northeast wall as this can create quarrels; any of the other walls are fine.

- Extractor fans are not auspicious in a kitchen. It is much, much better just to open the window to get rid of the cooking odours, like your Grandmothers used to. Only fit one if it is absolutely essential and make sure it is a quiet one. Kitchens have their own noise and they don't like vibrating fridges, squeaking washing machines or roaring extractor fans, so if any of your appliances are humming away to themselves get them repaired as soon as possible.

- The sink should be kept clean and unblocked, because the plumbing relates to your intestines and your finances, ergo blocked drains – blocked intestines and finances. The sink should always be placed against a window, and the best material for it to be made from is stainless steel which is a symbol of intuition and prosperity.

- Hang a crystal in the kitchen window as this attracts the energy and lifts it in the room (see the first cure, page 111).

Microwaves

I have to be careful talking about microwaves because I have strong feelings about them and I often upset people with my views, but I feel I wouldn't be doing my duty if I didn't mention them at all. They are one of my pet hates. When I studied oriental diagnosis and nutrition I noticed that when clients with a wide range of ailments followed the dietary recommendations but cooked in a microwave, the healing was much slower or didn't happen at all. But, as soon as they started cooking on a real flame they got better much more quickly. I believe microwaves can interfere with cell formation, they cook food from the inside out and they break up its whole metabolic nature.

If you have a microwave, get it checked regularly and keep plants (see the eighth cure, page 121) near it to absorb some of the electrical pollution, and if you are poorly, don't cook with it. But at the end of the day, I would be much happier if you got rid of it altogether.

Dining rooms

Don't let your dining room table become covered with papers and don't have too many ornaments around the room. They distract from the table, the conversation and the food.

The dining room should be square, round or octagonal, and as balanced as possible. If your dining room is rectangular or part of the sitting room, then you need to make a distinct divide between to the two rooms with a screen or something similar.

It is inauspicious to be able to see the toilet from the dining room as the vapours and the steam tend to seep into the room. I once went to a supper party at a small flat where the toilet was very much in view of the dining room. The walls were thin and it was rather embarrassing using the toilet in full view and earshot of the other diners. I was extremely self-conscious when I used the bathroom and put it off to the very last minute, and I don't

opposite: An oval-shaped table made from wood is perfect for dining off.

The view from this dining room is peaceful and tranquil. However, the flower arrangement is too tall for a dinner party and could create division among the guests.

The best colours for painting a dining room are pink, green or yellow, and look for a round or oval dining table that is made from wood as this has the most gathering influence. Make sure, too, that the chairs are as comfortable as possible as you don't want your visitors to leave the dining table too quickly. Further ways to improve the vibrations in a dining room are given overleaf.

Hang curtains at the window rather than blinds as they are more welcoming.

Make the centrepiece low and always burn candles in it.

Position quiet people at the head of the table facing the door as this will encourage them to be more garrulous.

Hang pictures on the walls of people eating and having a good time.

Large plants in the corner of the dining room are good for rejuvenating energy.

think I was on my own with this view. If your toilet is positioned in a similar place, do not embarrass your guests – send them to a different toilet.

It is also preferable that you don't see the kitchen from the dining room. If you have this situation, either hang a bead, fabric or chain curtain from the door frame to screen the view, or you can hang a small 20 mm (¾ in) crystal sphere from the top of the door jamb to improve the energy in the dining room.

The front door should not be visible from the dining room as it is distracting. Instead, the view from the dining room should be tranquil, or no view at all. If you are looking at a busy road, it is more difficult to relax, you will tend to move more quickly, and it will encourage you to eat fast and leave early.

Achieving good feng shui in a dining room

● Good colours for dining rooms are pink, peach, green or yellow and the room must be comfortably warm, but it should not have a real flame fire.

● Curtains are preferable to blinds because they create a calmer atmosphere.

● Fill the walls with pictures of people partying, dining and picnicking, and generally having a happy time at a gathering where eating is involved.

● Mirrors (see the first cure, page 111) have a wonderful influence in the dining room so use as many as you like. This and the bathroom are the only rooms that you can hang mirrors so that they are opposite each other. They bounce energy backwards and forwards which will result in stimulating conversation. It is not so beneficial for digestion, but it will help to create a wonderfully enjoyable supper party.

● The best shape for a dining room table is round or oval, the top should not be made from glass, otherwise when people see their legs they will feel like leaving. Also when they put anything on the table from a wine glass to an item of cutlery it will make a jarring noise which will embarrass your guests. Comfortable chairs are essential.

● Don't position the table so that there is a beam above it as this can make a divide between the guests.

● I have been to many dinner parties where there has been a magnificent, exotic, tall decoration right in the centre of the table. Unfortunately, this kind of arrangement will create a divide between your guests: if you cannot make eye contact easily it is difficult to start up a conversation.

- Tall candelabras are also divisive, and they are best placed on dressers or sideboards around the edge of the room as long as the light they are emitting is not as bright as your main table centrepiece.

- Place your quietest guests so that they are facing the main entrance into the dining room. This is known as the power seat and it will make them feel more confident and chatty. Guests who often take over the conversation can be placed with their backs to the door and it may make them a bit quieter. Your most honoured guest should also be positioned in one of the power seats.

A centrepiece that includes mirror, crystal and candles stimulates conversation and draws everybody close together.

Bedrooms

What do you think this room relates to? It is the most private place in the whole house and so relates to the most private part of you. It is the room in which you spend more time than any other, it is your sanctuary. A room where people only come in if they are invited.

Are you very open and is anyone allowed in your bedroom? Or do you keep the door closed behind you so no one can see? Would you be proud if we were to go in there now? Is it the last room that you decorated in the house? If it is, then you probably tend to put yourself last, too. If you wish to be treated with respect, you have to treat this room with respect because it represents the real you.

One of the best materials for a bedhead is wood.

The bedroom should be located at the back of the house, ideally situated in the far right-hand corner of the bagua, which is known as the relationship area. The energy in this area is the softest and most feminine in the whole of the house. The room needs to have an atmosphere of safety, warmth and nurturing. If it is also in the southwest, so much the better.

As usual, ensure there is no clutter in this room. If the first thing you see when you wake up in the morning is a pile of last night's clothes your immediate thoughts are 'I must clear those away' and this very thought makes you tired before you have even start your day. If you look in the wardrobe and see a pile of shoes, most of them looking worn, then throw out the ones you haven't worn for years. You probably won't even miss them. Some people have so many clothes that they genuinely do not know what is in their wardrobe and it is very tiring looking after that many clothes! Do you remember a time when you only had three dresses or one suit and a couple of pairs of jeans? And didn't you feel a lot lighter?

This is not the room to store books, keep those in the study, and it is definitely not a good idea to have an office in your bedroom. You will find that your bedroom things get confused with the office things; you will tend to start work before you get dressed, and you will not have as restorative a night's sleep as you might expect because your subconscious

Having somewhere comfortable to sit in your bedroom makes it even cosier and more inviting. Your bedroom is a place in which to be safe.

mind will be thinking about work. In an ideal world, you don't have anything in your bedroom except for the things listed on these pages. Your clothes should all be in a dressing room, which means that if you do come home late and you can't be bothered to put your clothes away neatly, or if you have gone out in a hurry and pulled everything out of your wardrobe, your bedroom will still be tidy. You can close the door on your dressing room and go to sleep with a semi-clear conscience.

Choosing and positioning your bed

It is usually better to sleep in a wooden bed, and have a mattress with natural fibres, and cotton or linen sheets. Synthetic fabrics interfere with the body's ability to 'breathe', they also create static electricity – several thousand volts can be generated by a small amount of movement and these currents are enough to interfere with the functioning of the body.

The perfect place for the bed is diagonally opposite the bedroom door. The headboard should always be against a wall. If it isn't, you can become insecure and less grounded. On a number of occasions I have met clients who have been sleeping with their beds 'floating' in the middle of the room. Some people do this because they read in a book that they ought to be sleeping with their heads pointing in a particular direction. There are directions which support you more than others, but the Compass School always takes the Form School into consideration first (see page 18). It is therefore more important to have a bed against a solid wall and to have it positioned correctly within the room than to be aligned in a favourable position.

If you have the headboard against a window it will damage your liver. If you have the headboard positioned so that half of the bed is against a window and half against a wall you will not only damage your liver but you will also become more insecure and feel less supported by one of your parents.

Never position the bed feet first directly lined up with the door. This is known as the coffin position and drains away your energy slowly but surely (especially if the door opens into an en suite bathroom). I have heard that some hospitals stipulate that beds should not be wheeled feet first out of the room because it is bad for the patients' health. If your bed is

Cleansing the bed

It is not always feasible to buy a new bed or mattress, but you can cleanse the mattress by burning a smudge stick (see page 128) all round the bed. Keep a bowl of chalk under the bed for 27 days, and then sprinkle holy water which you can get from the church (while using the three secrets – see the eleventh cure, page 125), and buy new bed linen.

To make a fresh start, it is advisable to change your bed every time a new cycle starts in your life, which is approximately every seven to nine years. Beds absorb more energy than most items of furniture because first we spend a third of our lives in them and second, while we are sleeping, we 'discharge' more. If you sleep with a new partner in a bed you previously shared with someone from a relationship that failed, it is more likely that your relationship will follow the pattern of the first.

in this position and you cannot move it, make sure you have a solid foot board and put a small bookcase, or wardrobe, at the bottom of the bed to slow down the energy. If you don't have enough space to do this, then hang a curtain and a 20 mm (¾ in) spherical crystal (see the second cure, page 112) from the door to disperse some of the influence. If the bed itself is lined up with an en suite bathroom door, tradition says this can cause severe financial loss or death, so avoid this position at all cost (see Bathrooms, page 86).

If you are too close to the door, you will find that your subconscious mind is always monitoring the door in case any one is about to come in, which will disturb your sleep and weaken your health.

Ceilings and beams

There should be no slanted walls, slanted ceilings or missing corners to your bedroom; it should be as balanced a shape as possible. Even more importantly, there should be no beams in the room. If there are beams across your bedroom ceiling they can create an invisible divide, cutting through communications. A beam running lengthways over the bed can cause immense problems between a couple.

The other affect beams can have is to adversely affect your health. If they are crossing over your bed the part of the body over which they are situated will become weaker.

A young girl had been sleeping in a bed which had a beam crossing over the region of her stomach. She had been in this house for about two years and working hard to save up for a year long trip to Africa. Within the first week of arriving in Africa she was struck down with an intestinal infection which was so bad that after a month she had to cut her trip short and she came home. She immediately went to the doctor and he prescribed some medicine. But even though she took the pills she saw no improvement and she went back and forth for months and the doctor could not understand why she was not healing. Eventually, he referred her to the hospital of tropical diseases but still she did not improve.

The girl then came across an article about feng shui and decided to take a consultation, and this is where I stepped in. By now it had been two years since she first caught the

A functional reading light that can be directed at will is the best choice for bedside table lighting.

In addition to living in a clutter-free space, it is
important that you position your bed in as
auspicious a place as possible (see page 64-5).
The best colours for painting a bedroom are
pink, red, purple, yellow, orange, lavender, peach,
terracotta or cream – the stronger the colour,
the stronger the influence. Further ways to
improve the vibrations in a bedroom are given
overleaf.

Stand a large plant in
the corner of your
room to freshen the
atmosphere.

Hang a spherical
faceted crystal in the
window to bring
more passion into
your relationship.

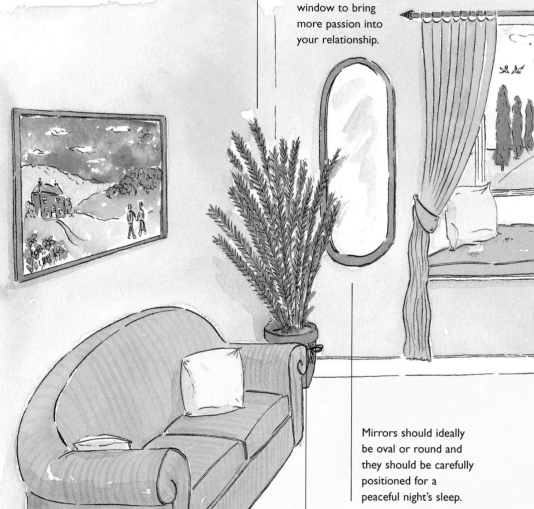

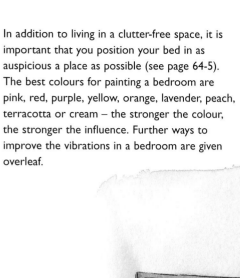

Mirrors should ideally
be oval or round and
they should be carefully
positioned for a
peaceful night's sleep.

Include a few small
items that contain
red, such as this red
ribbon tied around
the plant pot.

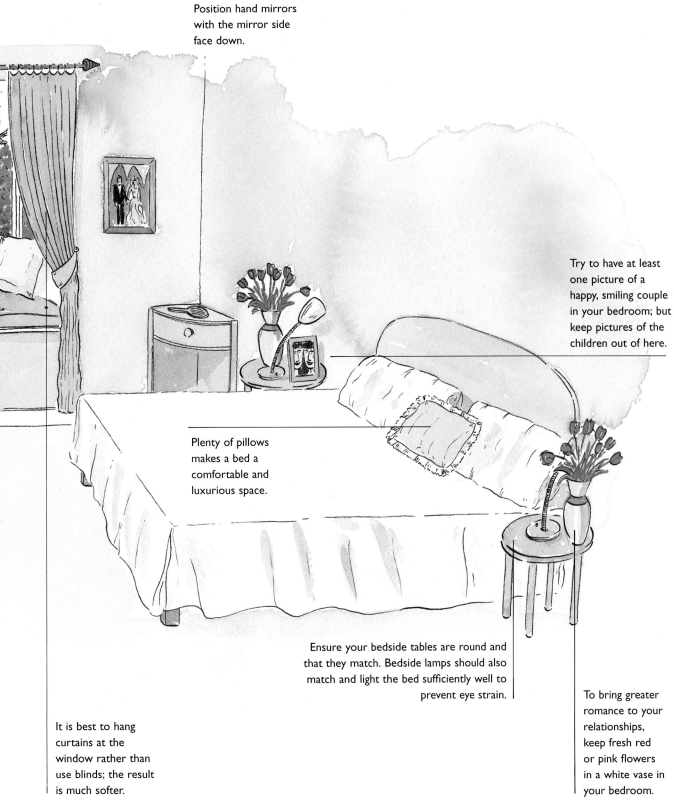

Position hand mirrors with the mirror side face down.

Try to have at least one picture of a happy, smiling couple in your bedroom; but keep pictures of the children out of here.

Plenty of pillows makes a bed a comfortable and luxurious space.

Ensure your bedside tables are round and that they match. Bedside lamps should also match and light the bed sufficiently well to prevent eye strain.

It is best to hang curtains at the window rather than use blinds; the result is much softer.

To bring greater romance to your relationships, keep fresh red or pink flowers in a white vase in your bedroom.

67

intestinal infection and with the passage of time she now had gynaecological problems, too. One of the first things we did was to move her bed from under the beam and within three months all the problems she had in the abdominal area healed.

This may seem like a miracle, but it can all be explained by science. First, sleeping under the beam had gradually weakened the area beneath it, which happened to be her stomach, to the extent that it had become the most vulnerable part of her. This meant that the first time she was exposed to the African bacteria she caught the infection quickly and violently. Second, when you are sleeping, your body is healing, your heart beat slows down, your breathing changes, and the body repairs itself, if it can. While she was sleeping beneath the constant pressure of the beam, the pills couldn't work because all her body could do was deflect the pressure with no energy left to heal, so the medicine was useless.

There is a form of 'beam in disguise' which has crept into the bedroom that you need to look out for. It is known as the overhead cupboard. Some fitted bedrooms have a

Directions for your head to point

The direction the bed should face depends on your flying stars, but the influences you will generally feel from each direction are outlined below.

I strongly recommend that you try each direction and experience the different influences for yourself. The direction that your head faces refers to when you are lying down and where the top of your head is pointing.

South Sleeping with the top of your head pointing towards the south is a good direction for someone who is involved in a lot of intellectual work, from writing or mathematics to studying for exams. This is my favourite sleeping direction.

Southeast Positioning your bed in a southeasterly direction will help you to absorb energy that is good for relationships and finances while you sleep.

East Sleeping with your head pointing towards the east tends to give you more energy and makes it easier for you to wake up in the morning. It can also improve your career prospects and financial situation. If you have difficulty waking up in the morning, put your pillow to the east for 27 days and you should find it much easier.

Northeast If your head is pointing northeast it can make you very ambitious, but can create a more disturbed sleep. If you put your bed in this position for 27 days it can make it easier to conceive children.

North Sleeping with the top of your head pointing towards the north promotes sound, healthy sleep. If you are having difficulty sleeping, then put your pillow to the north for 27 days.

Northwest The head pointing in a northwesterly direction can help you to create a family. This is also the direction that the head of a company should lay his or her head to receive more clarity and stronger organisational abilities.

West Sleeping with the top of your head pointing towards the west is a good direction for those that have retired, have been working too hard and are stressed, or if they are taking a sabbatical. It tends to give the sleeper a feeling of contentment.

Southwest If a bedhead is pointing towards the southwest it can create illness in its occupants and is not generally recommended.

wardrobe on either side of the bed (which send cutting chi towards the sleeper) and an overhead cupboard, so that the head of the bed is in a recess. This creates a pressure which is exerted onto your head and throat while you are sleeping. There is an especially nasty decorative feature which is often added to this design that hangs above the neck like a guillotine. This sends very powerful cutting chi, which can cause all sorts of neck and throat problems. The recess itself can cause headaches or brain problems. If you have this situation, take it down, or move the bed.

As we get older, our chi becomes weaker and it is harder for us to cope with bad feng shui, so if an elderly person slept in this bed they would become increasingly vague in the morning. Then they might start to complain of headaches and so on, whereas a child might not suffer any ill effects for a long time. It really is better not to have anything above your head, this includes everything from a slanted wall, to a heavy picture or a shelf.

Blue in the bedroom is very tranquil and the curtains are suitably soft and warming with their hint of pink.

Different types of bed

Metal beds can conduct geopathic and electromagnetic stress, if you absorb this while you are sleeping, it interferes with the body's ability to heal. Also for a lot of people, sleeping in a metal bed is a bit like sleeping in a cage. If you have a metal bed, tie some red ribbon on the bed to take away some of the metal energy.

Water beds are usually heated by metal coils. The water transmits the electrical field produced by these heating elements which interferes with normal sleeping patterns. Water and fire together are destructive.

Futons are one of the best designs for beds because they are made of 100 per cent natural materials, but it is a shame they are so low. Ideally, a bed should be between 60 and 75 cm (2 and 2 ½ ft) from the ground.

Four - poster beds or beds with a canopy can be difficult to get out of and lead to feelings of isolation. Round mattresses and beds lead to instability and brief relationships.

A bed piled high with white pillows is cosy and comfortable and the hinged bedside lamps mean that reading won't be a strain.

Different shapes of headboard

Arched headboards come from the metal element. This shape is auspicious if your date of birth makes you a metal person (see page 137) or if you are an accountant, administrator, lawyer or secretary, if you work in any capacity in an office, or if you are a martial arts expert, jeweller, financier, entertainer, salesperson, politician, guard, engineer, philosopher, or metal worker.

Square headboards are from the earth element. It is a lucky shape if you were born in an earth year (see page 137) or if you are an estate agent, teacher, potter, farmer, restaurateur, director of a charitable organisation, government official, prime minister, clergyman, actor, auctioneer, judge, scientist, policeman or a revolutionary.

Rectangular headboards belong to the wood element, so if you are a journalist, composer, surgeon, martial arts expert, explorer, forester, inventor, politician, master of ceremonies, carpenter, salesperson, broadcaster, film producer, television director, advertising executive, or stockbroker, or if your date of birth makes you a wood person (see page 137), it is a lucky shape for you.

Spiky headboards or those that are angular, star or triangular in shape relate to the fire element and so they are not generally recommended. With such a shaped headboard, life will increasingly become unpredictable and unstable and you may find it hard to go to sleep.

Wavy headboards belong to the water element, so if your profession is poetry, music, painting, entertaining, publican, diplomat, fisherman, thinker or a writer it is an auspicious shape.

A wavy headboard is an especially good shape if you were born in a water year (see page 137).

Mirrors

Mirrors are like a virtual reality and in bedrooms they can draw energy towards them and away from you. For the most peaceful, harmonious energy, only put round or oval mirrors in the bedroom (see the first cure, page 112). As an experiment, try propping up a mirror close to your bed so that you can see your reflection while you are reposing. You will find that you wake up at intervals throughout the night. While you are sleeping, your body is healing. All day you run around expending energy and when you go to sleep, your heart beat slows, your digestive system slows and the body repairs itself. When you have a mirror in the bedroom positioned so that you can see your reflection while you are lying in bed, it draws your energy towards it. This can slow down the healing process, because you are losing energy that your body would normally use for repairing the body. As a result, a mirror positioned like this can create bad health, insomnia or disturbed dreams.

Have you got mirrored wardrobe doors? If you have, and you can see your reflection in them from the bed, hang a curtain so that the mirrors can be screened off at night. And for those of you who have a mirror on the ceiling above the bed, I can almost hear you groaning at the prospect of taking it down. Well you don't have to. It is fine as long as it is very securely fitted and you screen it with a curtain or blind when it is time to go to sleep.

Do not leave hand mirrors or make-up mirrors facing up as they shoot energy out in an unstable fashion.

Achieving good feng shui in a bedroom

● Generally this area should be whatever shade you prefer, choosing from pink, red, purple yellow, orange, lavender, peach, terracotta or cream – the stronger the colour, the stronger the influence. Blue or black can be used in small amounts but grey, white, gold, or silver need to be used with care because they weaken the feminine energy.

● Try to incorporate at least a few red items in your bedroom; perhaps a picture, a red cushion or some red ribbon wrapped round something.

● Avoid stripes as they can create arguments and also avoid having strongly contrasting walls of colour, such as deep purple next to bright yellow, butting up against each other.

● The ceiling is best painted a paler colour than the walls. Dark ceilings shrink your energy field and can create stagnant energy.

A mayan ball hung from red ribbon deflects negative energy. Hang it in a window so you can see it from outside.

● Try to have at least one big plant in your bedroom to freshen the atmosphere. Large plants (see the eighth cure, page 121) are preferable because they have a stronger chi and they are less likely to look like clutter.

● Hanging a spherical faceted crystal (see the second cure, page 112) from a thread in the window brings more passion into your relationships.

● Don't have pictures of your children in your bedroom. Anywhere else in the house is fine but in your bedroom you need to forget that you are a parent and be a couple, or just you, again.

● Instead, in your bedroom have a picture of your wedding day or a photograph of both of you taken on an occasion when you and your partner were really happy, or a picture of two happy people. Enlarge the picture and hang it somewhere that you cannot miss it whenever you go to into the bedroom. Also, try to have warm, happy, safe pictures around the room to promote a feeling of safety.

● This room should have an atmosphere of softness and warmth, so curtains are preferable to blinds. Also, make your bed nest-like and sumptuous with lots of pillows – but not so many that your neck is uncomfortable.

● Don't have a television in the bedroom. If you must have one, get a cover for it or put it in a cupboard.

● The door should open into the room, and it should be able to open fully – so don't hang things on the back or pile things behind it, otherwise you will not be getting all the energy relating to your relationships that you should be receiving.

● Do not store anything – no winter clothes or bedding, books or magazines – under your bed. Keep it clear.

● It is best to have space on either side (to the right and left) of your bed so that neither you nor your partner feel as if they are cramped against a wall. The bedspread should not quite reach the ground so that there is a good circulation of fresh air around you.

● All furniture should be rounded, that means no sharp angled corners. You should have two matching bedside tables (even if you are single) and they should be round for good health and to prevent quarrels. If you have odd bedside tables it means that one of you will be more powerful than the other. Square or angular bedside tables can send out cutting chi that can be damaging to your health, especially the liver.

● You should have a matching functional bedside lamp on each bedside table. They need to shed a downlight, something like an anglepoise, so that you can read comfortably by the light.

● Halogen lamps (see the third cure, page 113) are often the best kind of light. Although they tend to use more electricity than conventional lights, they make up for it by having all the colours of the spectrum except infra red and ultra violet and they have a brighter, more concentrated, beam of light which tends to lift your spirits and combat seasonal affective disorder (SAD), to a degree. When you switch on a halogen lamp, the bulb turns from black to orange to white, mimicking the sun.

● Mirrors should be round or oval in the bedroom as they give off a more peaceful, harmonious energy. But you have to be careful where you hang them (see page 71).

● If you want to have a happy secure relationship, the bed should have a headboard that is in one piece and attached firmly to the bed (see also Headboards, page 70).

● If you normally sleep in cotton night-clothes and then you try sleeping in synthetic ones, you will notice that the sleep will not be as restorative. What we are sleeping in is always more important than what we wear during the day because we are healing while we are sleeping.

● Anyone who has ever lived in a cold house will have relished their electric blanket, and they are a wonderful invention, but don't sleep with them on because they can interfere with the body's delicate electro-magnetic system during that all-important time of healing. Good old-fashioned hot-water bottles are unbeatable.

● Never buy a mattress with a split down the middle if you want to have an active, warm and intimate relationship with your partner. A mattress that is divided in two suggests to your subconscious mind that there is an irreconcilable gap between you.

● To bring more romance into your life, keep a white vase with fresh red or pink cut flowers on the bedside table for 27 days, replenishing them as the flowers die, and then take a short break of about a week. Replace the flowers for another 27 days, and continue the cycle regularly.

Rooms for the poorly, or elderly loved ones

This room relates to an elderly person's own personal history. It is a place where we should pay respect to our ancestors because they gave us the gift of life. If a close, elderly member of your family is really happy right now, you will feel a bit happier. Conversely, if he is sad, then you will feel a little sad, too, because we are all linked together. So elderly loved ones should be especially well looked after, they are more vulnerable than we are, and they will feel the benefits of a harmonious bedroom especially strongly.

If an elderly relative, such as your Grandpa, moves into your house, make sure his room is empty before he moves in so that he can choose what will go in the room. Encourage him to decorate and personalise the area. It is important that he chooses the paint or wallpaper and helps, even if it is in a small way, to do the decorating. (Better not to decorate it as a surprise for him unless he has chosen the coverings.) Even though you are giving Grandpa free rein to decorate however he would like, positively discourage him from painting the room 'hospital green'. This particular green resonates with decay and, in oriental diagnosis, when this colour is seen in the complexion it indicates the possibility of cancer.

One of the difficulties will be moving from a house to a room as this will mean letting go of lots of furniture. Gently persuade him to bring only beautiful and useful things, for if the room is overstuffed it will feel cramped, depressing and reclusive. Furniture may have been inherited from a loving father, like a desk, which has huge sentimental value, but it may be considered ugly by everybody and never used and it will just form an obstacle as it blocks one end of the room. Your loved one should very gently be persuaded to sell it. We don't need pieces of furniture to remind us of departed loved ones, they are always linked to us. Make sure the door can open fully with nothing or very few things hung on the back or piled up behind it. If you really want something, find an item they wore very frequently like a pocket watch or a ring – this will contain more energy than a piece of furniture.

It is very good for your elderly relative to personalise the door to their room or suite, say, by putting on a different door handle. It is important because this has become a front door and it helps her or him to become more independent. If you have an ailing or elderly loved one, the room should face east or southeast to gain as much morning energy as possible.

Achieving good feng shui in an elderly relative's room

- Use strongly coloured towels to give the person more strength. Blue, pink and green are healing colours.

- Don't have any fluorescent lights (see the third cure, page 113). They seem to resonate at a particular frequency that is not particularly good for health and can cause headaches. Instead, use halogen bedside lamps. If your elderly relative is bed ridden, install a daylight bulb.

- On the wall in front of the bed hang a noticeboard with a picture of something relating to your relative's goals. Grandpa might want to take his grandchild to see a film next week so he might pin up an advertisement of the film. When the treat has happened, take down the picture. The noticeboard should never get cluttered.

- Arrange to have all sorts of pastimes like a radio, cassette player, pen and paper, knitting or jigsaw puzzles within easy reach to encourage activity.

- A visit from a healthy, loving animal has a wonderful healing energy.

- An aquarium (see the seventh cure, page 118) can bring more luck and life into a life. Don't keep it too near the bed, though, and make sure you have a pump and a filter to keep the water as clean as possible. A fish tank can start smelling unpleasant all too easily. And fix a mirror (see the first cure, page 111) behind the tank to double the energy of the fish.

- Try to keep the air fresh and sweet. So keep bedpans and potties under the bed or, even better, in a bedside cupboard out of sight. Also burn aromatherapy oils every day to keep the air smelling fresh. A continuous supply of fresh air is important, especially for those who don't get out very often. If it is too cold, an air filter is a good alternative.

- To stop energy becoming stagnant, hang a spherical faceted crystal (see the second cure, page 112) from a silver thread in the window. As the sun shines through the crystal it will cast colourful rainbows of sunlight in prisms all over the room at certain times which will encourage mental activity.

- See also the advice for bedrooms on pages 71-4.

It is important to have a happy photograph of your loved ones with members of the family to inspire feelings of contentment.

Children's rooms

This room relates to pleasure and joy, it represents the fruits of your labour, whether you have children or not.

Lots of clutter can make it difficult for your child to think clearly. They can become easily distracted, which will make it harder for them to find their vocation. If your child has lots of toys, books and clothes that have been grown out of, persuade them to take them to a charity shop or the local hospital. Bring your child with you to drop off the things – there is nothing nicer than giving, especially if your gift is really appreciated and you can get your child into the habit of letting go of clutter from an early age.

A child's room should not be at the front of the house nor in the centre (unless you want the children to be involved in every household issue!), and finally not at the back of the house. Ideally, they should be in one of the middle rooms, preferably one that is west-facing. If you have several children and have to use the back room, then give it to the eldest child.

Babies and small children like to have a nice safe, square or rectangular-shaped room

Soft toys, plenty of pictures, a warm carpet underfoot and pale colours are conducive to a calm and peaceful bedroom.

Paint a child's room
in pastel colours and
the effect is soft and
soothing. The wooden
bed is perfect for a
child to sleep in.

and they like to have two sides of their bed including the headboard against a wall. This makes them feel more secure. Preferably a baby should have his head pointing north or west with his feet pointing south or east to encourage a less interrupted sleep.

Teenagers benefit from irregularly-shaped rooms. These shapes encourage them to be more experimental and adventurous and find their own identity. Teenagers should sleep with their heads pointing south or east to make them sleep less!

As described on pages 65-9, the bed must not be situated under any over-hanging feature. If the bed is under a beam, a slanted ceiling, a shelf or a cupboard which crosses over the head end, it will make it more difficult for a child to get up in the morning. If there is a beam crossing over the body, it will make that area weaker and more susceptible to illness. Children have a very strong life force and generally feng shui shas will have a milder affect upon them than it would have upon an adult.

The bed should be wooden and the headboard needs to be fixed firmly to the bed and all the bedding should be of natural materials. A four-poster bed is not generally

In addition to making this as clutter-free a space as possible, it is important that you position the cot or bed in as auspicious a place as possible (see pages 64-5). The best colours for painting a child's bedroom are pale, pastel shades rather than too striking primaries. Further ways to improve the vibrations in a child's room are given opposite, and see also the bedroom information on pages 71-4.

The squarer the room the better as this is a safe shape.

Hang pictures of happy people around the room; at least one of them should feature pictures of the family.

To strengthen creativity, hang a spherical faceted crystal in the window.

Position the bedhead against the wall.

Hang any mobiles above the foot of the bed to prevent mishaps

A cot or bed made from wood is the best material as it is natural.

Have a round bedside table near to the cot or bed.

Keep a large plant in the room to freshen the atmosphere.

recommended for children as they will encourage your offspring to spend more time in bed, and can promote feelings of isolation.

Likewise, don't put your children in bunk beds. Not only is it very difficult to read a story and cuddle up comfortably when you are on a bunk bed, but the child in the bottom bunk is cramped and will not adapt so well into society, and the child in the top bunk becomes more insecure and ungrounded.

If the bed has a window behind the headboard is can make the child quarrelsome. If the headboard is half against a wall, the child will feel less supported by one parent than the other.

Achieving good feng shui in a child's room

● Colours that are appropriate for each room depend upon the child's individual flying stars (see pages 136-39), but generally it is good to use quiet colours to promote sleep – and be careful of too much red.

● A photograph with Mum and Dad holding their child in their arms looking very loving and protective close to the bed will promote a feeling of security. You may have to replace this photograph regularly since babies tend to kiss them till they dissolve and need replacing!

● Don't allow too many aggressive pictures. If your child is in their 'dinosaur' phase, balance them with more warm, friendlier pictures.

● The furniture in the room should be rounded and have no sharp corners, and the child should have a round bedside table to promote good health, prevent quarrels, and encourage reading.

● It is wonderful to have a light switch or a reading lamp on a bedside table within easy reach of the bed that the child can operate as this will encourage reading.

● Curtains are more auspicious than blinds. If you really want blinds, choose a roller blind first, then horizontal and finally vertical.

● If you are furnishing a baby's room, don't hang a mobile directly over your baby and certainly not over her head. Instead, locate it nearer to her feet where she will still be able to see it but it will not send out any cutting sha and there will be no danger of it dropping on top of her.

● If a child's bedroom has a television or a video in it, it will make it more difficult for the child to sleep because the energy in the room becomes more activity orientated than sleep-based. So keep the television in the sitting room or the playroom.

- If you have the luxury of a playroom, try to store nearly all the toys there. Playrooms should be painted in bright colours to stimulate mental activity. But no strongly contrasting stripes.

- If you don't have a playroom, encourage your children to put most of their toys in a cupboard or toy box at night.

- Bedrooms should be for sleeping and be full of softness, space and freshness. So don't have vivid pictures on the pillow because the child can tend to lose their identity and they will have a less refreshing sleep.

- Ensure that you have at least one big plant to freshen the atmosphere but make sure it has rounded leaves rather than spiky ones. So no yuccas!

- Encourage your children to personalise the doors to their rooms as they are the 'front doors' to their 'houses'. Also encourage them to treat each area of the bagua within the room (see opposite). For example, putting a light and some stuffed toys in the relationship area will help them to become more independent and responsible. Research has shown that children who establish a clear identity onto their rooms adapt more easily into society.

- Hang a spherical faceted crystal (see the second cure, page 112) in the window to make them more creative.

- It is very reassuring for a child to have a poem written as a border at the top of the wall, saying something like 'Once upon a time there was a tiny princess who made everybody smile and she lived in a room as blue as the sky [if the room is painted blue], and every night the stars and the moon looked down upon her and filled her dreams with happy laughter...' This will promote a feeling of security for the child and make her more inclined to make everybody smile!

- If the idea of painting a border is a bit daunting, then make a collage-type photograph of your child. Get it enlarged and draw a crown on his head and you could include a brother or sister, or both of the parents, and write something like: 'Once upon a time there was a little prince who made everybody smile lived with his mother and father the good king and queen in a room as yellow as a buttercup...etc.

- The best material to have on a child's bedroom floor is carpeting as this is the most comforting for a growing child or teenager.

Improving the feng shui in a child's room

In the relationship area, two or more cuddly toys.

In the wealth area, a money plant (see the eighth cure, page 121).

In the children's area, a crystal (see the second cure, page 112).

In the knowledge area, a boulder, collection of stones, or a statue (see the sixth cure, page 118).

In the fame area, a coveted cup or a copy of an examination result.

In the career area, a wind chime (see the fourth cure, page 114).

In the ancestor area, a picture of family.

In the helpful people area, another crystal.

The bedding on these matching beds doesn't quite reach the ground, allowing energy to circulate around the bedroom.

Bathrooms
and toilets

The bathroom is known in the East as the devil's room. The toilet relates to your health and your finances more than any other area in the house. It is a place of retreat and should therefore be a place where you are not going to be disturbed and a little way away from main areas of activity so that it can be as private as possible.

Rule number one: no, it's not clutter this time. The lid of the toilet should always be kept down. If you were to use a spray gun to colour the air around this receptacle, you

Feng shui approves of a screened toilet, natural flooring and cool, clean lines.

Round mirrors
accentuate creativity.

would see that all the air moves downwards via plug holes and the toilet towards the drains. When you flush the toilet, a large amount of energy gets 'sucked' downwards. By keeping the lid down, you can protect every facet of your life.

Once upon a time, toilets used to be at the bottom of the garden, but over the years they gradually crept closer and closer to the house until they were just outside the front door. Then they were put into the ground floor and, finally, upstairs. And now you will find an en suite in many homes. I have even seen houses that have a toilet concealed in a small wardrobe-type cupboard in the bedroom.

The positioning of the toilet within your home is very important. Good and poor places are described opposite and overleaf. Put down the lavatory seat before flushing to prevent all your energy disappearing down the drains. Further ways to improve the vibrations in a bathroom are also given overleaf.

Position the bath so that the bather's head faces the door – this is far less vulnerable than having your back to the door.

Ensure there is a window in the bathroom.

Mirrors are good in a bathroom, but keep them clean.

Large plants help to keep the atmosphere fresh and clean.

The best flooring is wooden floorboards, tiles or linoleum.

It is disturbing for a feng shui consultant to see how many new bathrooms and toilets are now put into houses. The goal appears to be to have one toilet for each member of the family, one for the gardener or workmen, and one for visitors! This is too many bathrooms for the average house and over time they will weaken the health of the residents.

Bathroom and toilet location
The best place to locate a bathroom or toilet is in the ancestor, helpful people, career or children area. The lavatory is also made more auspicious if it is screened from the door.

ROOM LOCATION Above the front door.

RESULT Can be disastrous for everyone.

CURE Relocate the room or hang a bagua mirror (see the first cure, page 111) on the reverse of the toilet door. The mirror will gather and deflect the chi so that the family's finances are not flushed straight down and out of the front door. Keep a heavy stone, concrete or earthen pot, or statue (see the sixth cure, page 118) in the room to slow down the movement. Also keep a money plant (see the eighth cure, page 121) there and use a high-wattage up-light.

ROOM LOCATION In the centre of the house with no external windows.

RESULT Ill health and not being able to complete projects.

CURE The best option is to relocate the room, and the next choice is to hang a bagua mirror on the reverse of the toilet door shining towards the hall to protect your health. Do not let the room become cluttered. At least once a week, during the day, when the house is being cleaned, plug in an electric fan in the bathroom for an hour to disperse the malignant steam and vapours and burn an aromatherapy burner.

ROOM LOCATION Opposite the front door.

RESULT Money and opportunity comes in and goes straight out.

CURE Hang a bagua mirror on the reverse of the toilet door so that it is shining towards the front door.

ROOM LOCATION In the wealth area.

RESULT Money drains away.

CURE   Hang a bagua mirror on the reverse of the toilet door above eye level shining out towards the hall or install a fish tank (see seventh cure, page 118) or symbols of fish, up-lights and a money plant (see the eighth cure, page 121).

ROOM LOCATION   In the relationship area.

RESULT   Poor health and short-lived relationships.

CURE   Hang a bagua mirror on the reverse of the toilet door shining into the hall or install a pair of stone, concrete or pottery statues (see the sixth cure, page 118) (rabbits are specially auspicious – see the seventh cure, page 118), up-lights, a money plant (see the eighth cure, page 121), a spherical faceted crystal (see the second cure, page 112) and burn an aromatherapy burner or a candle (see the third cure, page 113) regularly.

ROOM LOCATION   Attached to the bedroom as an en suite, or in the same room as the bedroom.

RESULT   Poor health and bad luck.

CURE   First of all, don't line up the bed opposite the toilet door and hang a 20 mm (¾in) crystal from a red ribbon from the door frame. Keep plants (see the eighth cure, page 121) in the bathroom and regularly burn an aromatherapy burner.

ROOM LOCATION   Above or next to the kitchen.

RESULT   Poor health.

CURE   Hang a 20 mm (¾ in) spherical crystal from a thread of red ribbon from the top of the door jamb between the two rooms, and keep plants in the bathrooms to absorb the steam and vapours.

Achieving good feng shui in a bathroom

● Try to position the room in either the ancestor, helpful people, career or children areas of the bagua.

● Make sure your bathroom has a window which opens easily, as the bathroom needs good ventilation.

● Double basins are preferable to single ones.

● Ceramic tiles are the best choice of floor covering as they belong to the earth element and control water.

Keep the toilet door (or bathroom door if this is where your lavatory is) shut all the time to contain the energy within the room – unless you are spring cleaning and all the windows are open in the house.

You can hang mirrors (see the first cure, page 113) facing each other on directly opposite walls as this helps to open up the space in what can very frequently be a small room.

Try to position the bath so that the end furthest from the taps faces the door.

The heart-shaped mirror hanging above the bath allows the bather to see who is coming in and promotes a feeling of security.

Studies

*Feng shui prefers
cupboards for storage
but if this is
impossible for you, use
storage containers to
keep the inevitable
piles of paper at bay
in the office.*

To have a small business running from your home which involves having a desk, filing cabinets, telephones and possibly staff, and takes up more than 36 hours a week, is not recommended for good feng shui. But a study is a different matter all together. It can be a vitally useful room, the children can do their homework here, you can keep all your hobby related things, and you can do all your household paperwork here. It is best situated near the front of the house or in the northeast room as this is a good area in which to study.

As ever, you need to keep the space as clutter-free as possible. All offices should be

treated like presidents' offices, don't let them be used as 'dumping rooms'. This is the room where you are going to make your fortune, so don't let the energy get stagnant, keep it flowing. If your desk is buried under a pile of paperwork it will make you feel tired and depressed before you start your day. Looking for lost paperwork costs hours every week. Be ruthless and throw out as much as you can. Most people find themselves working in a little area the size of a postage stamp so you need to be really firm with clutter.

When I am working on a project, my desk gets piled with research material, but at lunch time and at the end of the day I clear it all away – I have a file for everything. If I am planning to go on holiday to Canada I start a new file, called 'Canada' and I put everything relating to the trip in that file. When I return from the holiday I throw away the file. On my desk we have one very important A4 book and in it is recorded every telephone call and query that we receive throughout the day, there is also an area ruled off to explain whether we have dealt with the query or not. This keeps all our queries to one book. File it, put it on the computer, deal with it, or bin it. Everything you put off until later takes away your energy, whether it is a phone call, a letter or some filing. Don't wait, do it straightaway. If you clear your desk every night it will psychologically brighten your morning the next day. Take a couple of days to clear your office and it will pay off, you will be more organised and efficient, and you will feel less tired. Also, by letting something go, you make room for something new to come!

In fact, stop reading. Let's take advantage of the moment, take a couple of minutes to walk through your home or office and let some clutter go. Even if it is just one item – do it right now and start a habit of a lifetime.

Furnishings made from natural materials like wood are preferable and the rounded edges to this work surface will prevent money from slipping off. Having your back exposed, however, is never desirable in feng shui.

Positioning the desk

Your desk should be positioned so that you are sitting with your back against a solid wall with a good view of both the door and the window. There should not be enough room for someone to walk behind you while you are sitting at your desk, and don't store anything behind you that other people need to have access to on a regular basis. It's very irritating when people are constantly 'fussing' behind you and as you get annoyed you send out an aura of irritation that infects the whole room.

Your desk should not have a window or a mirror (see the first cure, page 111) behind it. Nor should it be too close to a window or you will find that every time a bird or an aeroplane flies past or a pedestrian walks by, you will be distracted by the movement. You should also not have a mirror opposite your desk or you will be constantly distracted by your own movements in the reflection, and, as you know, mirrors draw energy towards them which can deplete you in this situation.

In addition to working in a clutter-free space, it is important that you position your desk so that your back isn't facing the door. The best colour for painting a study is green with only the smallest amount of red – too much red and you will become restless. Further ways to improve the vibrations in a study are given overleaf.

If you must have blinds, ensure they are horizontal rather than vertical.

Have a bright reading lamp on your desk so that you can see everything clearly.

Keep red fresh flowers on your desk to promote clear thinking.

A crystal paperweight is useful, but keep it at least 1 m (1 yd) away from any electrical equipment as it emits as well as absorbs electrical vibrations.

Keep a healthy green plant in the office to absorb electrical pollution.

Have a fish tank or indoor fountain in the corner of the office.

Keep all your papers neatly stored in a filing cabinet to keep as much clutter at bay as possible.

Have a wooden desk preferably with curved edges.

Keep your book shelves low-level and not over-filled to keep them as unimposing as possible.

Glass paperweights can strengthen intuition; an invaluable asset, whatever your work.

If you have something in your office that is brighter or has a stronger energy than your desk lamp, like a fire or a television, you will find yourself constantly distracted. If there is a fire, you may find yourself getting up to stoke it, put on another log, or you may find you just keep looking at it. If there is a television and it constantly catches your eye, it will make you think about what you will watch later and you may find yourself watching when you should be working.

Achieving good feng shui in an office

● Colours that are auspicious for this room are usually green and red (although red should always be used in moderation as this can cause stress).

● The desk should generally be wooden although this is dependent upon your element as related to the flying stars (see page 137).

● If you are working with creative concepts, ensure your desk is rounded. But if you are dealing with very precise concepts or doing a lot of figure work, square is best but still with very slightly rounded corners; in feng shui we say that if your desk has right angles, your money will slip off the edge.

● Keep a bright, functional desk lamp on one side of your desk. This makes a pool of light on the desk which helps to keep your attention in this area.

● If your employer will not stretch to supplying an anglepoise for your desk in the office, then bring one in from home. Not only will you be improving the working environment, but you will be getting rid of some clutter from home.

● Sometimes I light a candle (see the third cure, page 113) on my desk. The extra gathering energy of the fire tends to keep me at my post until the task is finished.

- Fluorescent strip lighting (see the third cure, page 113) resonates at a frequency that can create headaches. It is much better to disable the light by taking out the tube and investing in a bright up-light as this will improve the atmosphere no end.

- Keep fresh cut flowers on one side of your desk all the time. They stimulate mental activity and cleanse the atmosphere. If your desk is wooden, red is the most auspicious colour. Buying flowers for work may seem like an unjustified expense, but if you think about it, you probably spend a minimum of 35 hours a week in your study and not only do flowers brighten up the area but they absorb electrical pollution, depression and negativity. So, it is worth spending a couple of pounds a week. And they are just as auspicious for men as they are for women!

- Studies have become very electrically charged places. In feng shui, generally the rule is one BIG plant per item of electrical equipment – small plants (see the eighth cure, page 121) can constitute clutter. Palms, peace lilies and spider plants absorb the most electrical pollution. They also absorb some of the poisonous solutions that we use in construction materials.

- It is generally auspicious to have an indoor water fountain (see the seventh cure, page 118) to freshen and de-ionise the office.

- Generally, don't have pictures of your children, golfing trophies or hobbies around your study. These things distract you and cause you to waste time in this room. Instead, it is helpful to hang up pictures of your goals, related work or current projects.

- Keeping a crystal paperweight (see the second cure, page 112) on your desk can strengthen your intuition, but make sure it is at least 1 m (1 yd) from your computer as it absorbs and radiates electrical pulses.

- It is better to have only low-level shelving and storage otherwise you can have the impression that everything is coming down on top of you. Shelves should never be 'jam packed' full. Instead, there should be room for more books or files to come in. Store the heaviest books on the bottom shelves and ensure that these shelves are slightly more full than the ones above.

- Hang a small metal wind chime (see the fourth cure, page 114) just inside your office door to promote clear thinking, and bring in more opportunity.

- Choose your window dressings in this order: curtains, roller blinds and, lastly, horizontal blinds. Vertical blinds are not regarded as auspicious.

Gardens

The Japanese were the first recorded people to cultivate a garden purely for aesthetic reasons. They believed gardens were sacred places where you went to meditate and recover from the stresses of the day. Gardens play a very important part in feng shui and in China there are documents recording that gardens have been laid out within feng shui guidelines for more than 3000 years.

Gardens designed within the principles of feng shui should take into account some of the following:

Judiciously placed statues or boulders can create stillness and tranquillity in a garden.

- Positioned around the garden should be something from the fire element, perhaps a lamp; something from the metal element, that could be a statue or a boulder; something from the water element, and something from the wood element like a tree, shrub or plant.

- There should be something textured and something smooth, something soft and something hard, light and shade, short and tall. Feng shui is concerned with seeking balance by contrast so something that is still like a rock next to something that is fluid like water can make a more harmonious ambience. The best possible place to have a garden is in front of a great lake with a large mountain behind because then you will have an equal contrast of fluidity and stillness.

- Houses are generally made of hard straight lines so we need the contrast of curves and softness in the garden to keep this balance.

The entrance, whether a drive or path, to the garden needs to be carefully planned in order to maximise opportunity and harmony. It should be wider at the road side and gradually getting narrower and meandering towards the house like an old lazy river. Ideally,

you should place something heavy on either side of the entrance to the grounds to prevent your luck from running out. In traditional European gardens, greyhounds or griffins holding shields or lions, might have been used in place of fu dogs. The pair should look a bit ferocious in order to discourage any would-be burglars (see also The entrance to your world, pages 38-41).

It is delightful to have a secret summer house, hidden away in the grounds, an inviting place whose use is not restricted to the warmest summer months. In China, this garden pavilion would be round, five-sided, which represents the five elements, or eight-sided, which represents prosperity. It should have facilities to make a hot drink, heating and light. It needs its own private garden which would be low-maintenance so you can come here to relax not to dig and hoe! It should have an outside light carefully situated to show the garden to its best advantage and a tree or plant specifically chosen to strengthen your health, and a water element. Don't fill the summer house with lots of things as this will take away your energy through tidying or dusting. The summer house should be minimalist so you can relax and contemplate your garden without distraction.

Elegant pagodas with their varying number of floors and pointed roofs are not a common sight in the West, but they improve the quality of the feng shui for the whole area. They are generally placed in the southwest or the northeast corner to neutralise the spirit energy in those areas.

Evergreen plants symbolically represent longevity and a summer house can be an inviting place if you are in search of peace and quiet.

Position the bagua on your garden just as you would inside the home and then put items relating to the five elements in each area to enhance the feng shui (see opposite). When choosing your plants, look for a contrast of textures but do not have too diverse a choice of colours. Further ways to improve the vibrations in a garden are given opposite and overleaf and see also the entrance to your home on pages 40-41.

A summer house or pagoda is a wonderful retreat; keep it stocked with books and games.

Some water in your garden enhances its feng shui. The siting of the water feature will depend on the orientation of the house.

Combine areas of well-cultivated garden with wilder places.

If you have a fence running along one side, make sure it is shaped with a happy 'smile' along its top edge.

Garden furniture should be comfortable, so try to use all-weather upholstery.

Keep a bird feeder in the garden to attract more wildlife.

Paths should have gentle curves and should be narrower near the house.

Applying the bagua to the garden

Just as the bagua is laid over a floor plan of your home, it can be positioned over a plan of your garden so that you can determine the different areas. Keep a statue or statuette of a dragon in the east, a tiger in the west a tortoise to the north and a red bird, crane or heron to the south (see the seventh cure, page 118).

The children area
is the perfect area for displaying something innovative like dramatic sculptures, a maze, or a collection of wind chimes (see the fourth cure, page 114) – look for something out of the ordinary. If you have children, this is the place to put the swing or the sandpit. The best colours for plants in this area are white, lavender, all the pastel colours, orange, yellow, blue or silvery.

The relationship area
of the garden is a good place to have a love seat or an arbour, and the main colours should be red or pink. This should be a quiet, romantic area, perhaps with fragrant flowers. Standing something heavy like a pair of statues (see the sixth cure, page 118) will keep relationships stable; a bird feeder gives relationships more chi.

The knowledge area
is a good place for a small table and chairs. You could also place a boulder or a statue here.

The benefactors area
will benefit from either earth or metal cures (see page 136), so a very small metal wind chime (see the fourth cure, page 114) (if you have a big garden and your neighbours are quite far away) or a sun dial would improve the energy in this area.

Achieving good feng shui in a garden

● A garden that is a riot of colour with all manner and style of plants would not be approved of in a garden designed to feng shui recommendations. The Chinese would say 'The five colours blind the eye' and they would prefer a more subtle approach. The colours that are most frequently used are delicate hues of white, especially in the shape of blossoms. If a vibrant colour were to be used, it would only be in very small amounts. Less is more.

● If there is something threatening the house like a large building overlooking it, for example, the garden forms a powerful defence and can protect the occupants. Plant an evergreen hedge around the periphery, or a copse of trees at a strategic point, to form a barrier and absorb and slow down a 'poison arrow', or fast-moving sha. Plants and water can create vital earth chi which surrounds the house with positive energy.

● A deciduous hedge has a different energy from an evergreen and symbolises weakening health and finances.

● It is considered auspicious to have a hill at the back of your house at the bottom of the garden. In a city this might take the shape of a building.

● You should never be able to see the garden all in one glance but be led from one area to another. Some of the garden should be carefully cultivated while some of it left natural to create a balance. The careful placement of rockeries can be used to prevent energy in the form of finances or health from slipping away. Traditionally, they would be located to the north of the garden, near the pond or at the bottom of the garden.

Waterfalls can improve your finances and it is always good to have flowing water nearby, but make sure it isn't flowing away from the house.

● Paths should have gentle curves, and be narrower at the house, becoming gradually wider as you go into the garden. Most of the paths should be found in the western part of the garden and they should be quite narrow to encourage you to be quiet and contemplate.

● Trees should be primarily planted in the east or southeasterly areas. Traditionally, all cultures from the ancient druids of Britain to the South Americans, the North Americans to the Balinese, had a respect for trees. Trees have often been there longer than you or me and have interacted with the chi and become one with it, and sometimes these trees behave like acupuncture needles and release pressure in the land. It is also said that spirits and divas live in trees and you need to ask them to leave before you can cut down a tree. It is much better to get a tree surgeon to trim the branches to stop the roots getting too big and disturbing the foundations or to grow a creeper up the tree or dress it up with fairy lights or something similar, to make the tree more appealing to you. Certain trees and plants are more auspicious than others (see the eighth cure, page 121).

● If you are lucky, you will have a stream that is flowing eastward.

● A water element will attract wildlife and it can dramatically improve your wealth by its judicious placement. Water is regarded as the life blood of a garden as it cleanses and revitalises the immediate area., and improves your luck.

● Encourage all wildlife into the garden from butterflies to birds (see the seventh cure, page 118). They bring more 'life energy' with them and they are also an indication that there is no serious pollution in that area.

● Add to the atmosphere in a garden by having your favourite poem etched onto a stone or a piece of wood, and hung somewhere slightly out of sight so that you can discover it as you round a corner. The poem needs to be synonymous with the atmosphere you would like to create. One of my favourites is:

> 'The buttercup catches the sun in its chalice
> and there's never a leaf nor a blade too mean
> to be some happy creature's palace.'

by *James Russell Lowell*

Choosing a new home

To find the perfect home, you must first look in the right direction (see Directionology, pages 132-5) because every time we move more than 1 ½ miles our energy is influenced, and if we move house, go on holiday or on a business trip that involves a long journey, then our energy is influenced especially strongly. When you move in a direction that is good, everything comes to you easily, but you can move in a direction which results in arguments, financial problems, ill health and separation. Different directions are auspicious at different times. When you move house, the influence can last from three to 20 years, so it is important to move in the right direction. That is step one.

Step two: the direction of the front door. Generally, a home that is south or southeast facing is favourable. The home will be filled with a sunnier, brighter energy as you 'walk it in'. Also, if your home is facing in a southerly or southeasterly direction you will find that the front rooms (which are most likely to be the sitting room and the kitchen) will have a much brighter, more active energy in them, which is ideal. Bedrooms should always

A home looking over views of water can make it easier to find your vocation. It also helps to have it facing south because energy is then more active.

be located at the back of the home and if the home is facing south they will be getting a more northerly energy which is quieter and makes it easier to sleep. I once tried to turn a north-facing room into a studio that I could paint in but I found I kept dragging all my equipment into the south-facing room because it had a much brighter, more active energy. When I painted in the south-facing room, my partner and even the cat used to come and join me. When I was in the north-facing room, no one came to visit.

Step three: always find out what happened to the people who lived there previously; as the predecessor chi will continue to have an effect on the home. For

example, did they move to a bigger house or were they forced to sell? Homes tend to have a history which repeats. For example, a couple might move into a house, be happy for a year then have a quarrel. She moves out and the man lives there for the next ten years on his own and then he decides to sell. Another couple buy the house and they live there happily for six months, then they have a row and she moves out and he lives there for the next thirty years. Conversely, a house can have a very happy history where all previous occupants have sold to move to a bigger property. By considering the history of the previous occupants you can get an indication of what is going to be the likely influence upon you and your family (see also pages 12-13).

Step four: consider the energy of the neighbourhood by looking carefully at your neighbours. Each different area has a different energy and supports a certain sort of person and occupation. This is why you will find bankers in one area, artists in another, and jewellers in another. Make sure the area suits your personality.

Your home should be slightly bigger or the same size as the others in the street. The best kind of property to live in is a bungalow, as you will then receive more of earth and heaven's energy. It also means that as your house is shorter it will cast less shade on the back garden. Generally, there should be lots of daylight coming in through the windows, so keep plants cut back and don't erect out buildings too close to the house.

This lovely wooden house with each floor the same size is one of the best shapes to look for.

101

A green and healthy garden is a good sign, especially if there are plenty of birds and butterflies around, too.

Look for water in the shape of rivers and ponds or lakes near the house. They need to be flowing and clean and ideally in the wealth area of the garden or at the front of the house. Make sure the water is not flowing away from the house.

At the back of the house there should be a hill to protect the occupants; if you live in a city this could be in the form of another house. To the east, look for a forest or a craggy hill that is not as high as the one at the back and larger than the one to the west. In an urban area, this might be your next door neighbour's house. To the west, there should be a hill or a house smaller than the one to the east. The west represents the white tiger, or the negative flow of energy, and it is said that if it is too large, the green dragon of the east will not be able to control him and he will devour the occupants of the house (see the seventh cure, page 118)!

When you see the house for the first time, be vigilant and note whatever you see during the journey. For example, if when you are approaching the property you stop your car and pause to look at a road sign and someone courteously approaches you and offers assistance you can take this as a good omen. Conversely, if you see an animal that has been run over, or someone beeps their horn because you are driving too slowly for their taste, these can be bad omens. The river (which is in this case a road) is flowing too fast, hence the dead animal and the impatient driver.

If, during the final part of the journey and when you arrive at the house, you see no wildlife and there is a dead bird in the garden it may be an indication of too much industrial pollution – not auspicious signs. If the garden is full of song birds, butterflies, rabbits or any healthy wildlife (see the seventh cure, page 118) and the garden is verdant and green, it can be a healthy sign.

After looking at the feng shui of the environment, the next most important consideration is the shape of the house. Ideally, the house should be a balanced shape, with each level above the ground floor approximately the same size. A balanced, even shape is associated with harmony, stability and cooperation among the occupants. See the descriptions of extended and missing areas on pages 21-29 for more information. Ideally, there should be no exposed beams or columns. Auspicious house shapes include:

● A dome-shaped roof is good because the curves gather energy. This shape is regarded as the best defence against negative energy.

● A square-shaped house belongs to the earth element and is a good, stable shape to live in.

● A round house belongs to the metal element and is also favourable.

● A rectangular house has good feng shui as it belongs to the tree element.

Things to avoid

● Before you purchase your home, it is well worth taking the time to check something we didn't have to worry about before the Second World War: the vicinity of toxic waste processing plants, nuclear power stations, or toxic land fills. I wouldn't want to live within ten to fifty miles of one of the above, depending on the direction of the prevailing winds. If I had the misfortune to live near a land fill area that contained cows that had died from BSE, for example, I would check the flow of the water table, and make sure my family and I were well above it. Also check where the electrical generators, transformers, big pylons and underground railway stations are. I wouldn't want to live within half a mile of one of those.

● After mentioning those things it seems a bit trivial to worry about trees! But trees should not be directly in front of the front door creating a gloomy entrance.

● Avoid properties with a toilet or bathroom opposite the front door. This can adversely influence your finances. A toilet or bathroom in the centre of the house and with no windows can be detrimental to your health, and in the area to the far right of the house, a bathroom can negatively affect your relationships, and finally if you have a bathroom in the far left-hand corner, it can block finances (see also pages 82-7). The location of the bathroom need not be a major problem, however, as long as you can get planning permission to relocate it.

● The road should be curving around the front of the house, not around the back. Avoid properties that have poison arrows in the shape of roads, rivers, bridges, railways or buildings pointing directly at them.

● It is particularly undesirable if a house or house plot has any triangular shaped parts (other than the roof), as a destructive energy is carried in the triangle. It has more acute corners than other shapes and so can collect stagnant and malevolent chi. Triangular shapes are also said to constrict and suffocate the occupants of the house.

● It is considered bad feng shui if the upper floors are larger or a lot smaller than the ground floors. It creates an unbalanced energy and things can happen that are beyond the control of the occupants. Likewise, long, thin towers or chimneys that are part of the house attract negative energy; the Chinese say they are fighting the sky.

A square-shaped house is a good and stable shape that belongs to the earth element. Large windows allow plenty of light and energy to flow in – but remember to keep them clean!

● Walls that are slanted or lean can create instability and occupants can be in danger of bankruptcy.

● Do not have three or more doors in a row, especially if they are in a straight line. Ideally, you should have a ratio of not more than three windows to each door.

● A terraced roof, or one that slants all the way down to the ground, gives the impression that the building is falling or slipping and residents can tend to lose money.

● Rooms that are cut off from the rest of the house, even if they are joined by a covered walkway, are considered inauspicious. An L-, H- or U-shaped house is also undesirable. Do not have split level floors, particularly if the dining room or kitchen is lower than the sitting room because you need a higher vibration in the kitchen.

● A house should not be built on sloping foundations or every facet of life can be unstable.

This round house belongs to the wood element and would be a good house for an artist to live in.

● A glass house or one that is a very uneven shape belongs to the water element and is not good to live in.

● Avoid a property that has had a fire more than once as it is probably fire prone.

● Don't live in a basement. Roads are regarded as rivers and if you live in a basement you are below the level of the water, which can lead to health problems and limited opportunity.

● Don't live in a house that has a hill or a steep slope in front of it.

● Avoid houses with beams or sloping ceilings, and if you are tall, avoid houses that have low doorways and ceilings.

● Avoid houses with spiral staircases; they weaken health.

● Don't live near a lunatic asylum, hospital, police station, church or graveyard. Around these buildings people will be experiencing a lot of pain, bitterness, anger, sorrow and depression and these strong emotions build up and envelop your house. When we feel an intense emotion like sorrow, that energy fills our auras and we radiate sadness and it infects everyone near us. Think of the last time you went out with someone who was very depressed, and how their energy changed the whole atmosphere.

Refining your feng shui skills

The nine basic cures

There are many more than nine basic cures but we call them nine (and occasionally eight) because eight and nine are auspicious numbers and on pages 111-25 we look at the most useful ones. So what are they? Well, cures can enhance energy, strengthen it, redirect it, slow it down or absorb shas – threatening elements. Basically, they are concerned with manipulating chi, or energy, to improve life and make it more harmonious.

Types of cure

An enhancement cure   might be used when you need to bring extra energy into a particular area while you are looking for a new job, or studying for an exam.

A permanent cure   would stay up all the time and is used if, say, you had a missing area to your home.

A protective cure   would also stay up permanently or until the sha went away. The sha might be anything from scaffolding pointing at your house to neighbours who send you psychological attacks, and its job would be to deflect and transmute the negative influences.

YIN	YANG
moon	sun
cold	hot
negative	positive
still	moving
soft	hard
loose	tight
gentle	rough
feminine	masculine
tall	short
black	white

The five elements

To select a cure, you have to be familiar with the five elements. The universe comprises of matter which can be identified as being either water, wood, fire, earth or metal. How these elements react together will dictate how they develop and influence everything around them, including you and me. Furthermore, each of these elements was born out of different mixtures of yin and yang: without man and woman we could have no children, without black and white there would be no grey. Yin and yang are the polar opposites, positive and negative extremes of everything in the universe, and some examples are listed to the left.

The qualities of each element

Wood (or tree) represents all living things, especially plants, and it is associated with spring, growth and activity, and with the east and southeast. It has an upward and more yang energy.

Fire symbolises expansion, burning, bright light and heat, and it is associated with summer and the south, and it has an expansive, upward, outward and the most yang energy.

Earth symbolises the centre, the middle line. It has a settled energy and it is associated with the periods between the seasons, a time of completeness. The directions are the centre, southwest and northeast and it has a stable, balanced energy of things beginning to settle. The earth energy is balanced between yin and yang.

Metal represents maturity, contraction and stability. It represents autumn and harvest time, and the direction is northwest and west, the energy is of contraction. This force is more yin.

Water is associated with all liquids from fog to the sea, and the rebirth and rotting down of everything. It is associated with winter and the north, which is not supportive of life. It is a time of hibernation, and the energy moves in a dissolving, spreading, seeping way and is the most yin.

Each of these elements is associated with an area of the bagua:

● Area no. 1: the career area – water

● Area no. 2: the relationship area – earth

● Area no. 3: the ancestor area – wood

● Area no. 4: the wealth area – wood

● Area no. 5: the health, or tai chi, area – earth

● Area no. 6: the benefactors area – metal

● Area no. 7: the children area – metal

● Area no. 8: the knowledge area – earth

● Area no. 9: the fame area – fire.

To select which cures are to be applied to each area we also need to know how the cycles of energy flow. First there is the creative cycle, the cycle of birth. This is represented as follows:

1   The **tree** energy feeds fire by creating fuel for the flames.

2   When the **fire** dies down, it leaves ash which turns into earth.

3   As time passes, the contraction of the **earth** compounds it into rocks and then into metal.

4   When the **metal** gets cold it creates condensation which creates water.

5   **Water** feeds the plants and trees.

Other cycles include the destructive cycle:

1   **Metal** cuts tree down.

2   **Fire** melts metal.

3   **Water** puts out fire.

4   **Earth** muddies water.

5   If you think of a house plant in a flower pot, after a while the **'tree'** exhausts the soil.

and the weakening cycle:

1   Too much fire will burn up all the **tree**.

2   Too much tree will drink all the **water**.

3   Water will rust the **metal**.

4   Metal will make the **earth** vanish as it becomes rock.

5   Too much ash (earth) puts out the **fire**.

Everything is divided into the five elements, some items from each element are listed below:

water	wood	fire	earth	metal
blue	green	red	yellow	white
fountain	plants	candle	statue	clock
aquarium	chair	pyramid	terracotta pot	crystal
glass	music	horse	dog	chicken

Therefore, if you were looking for a harmonious cure to strengthen an earth area, like the relationship or knowledge areas, you might choose something from the fire element, which would be a candle or an item containing red.

The first cure: mirrors

Mirrors are often included in the 'cure category' of light because chi behaves a little bit like light. With the aid of mirrors, chi can be captured, intensified or deflected.

Mirrors are very powerful, they are like a virtual reality and they draw energy towards them. The general rule when using a mirror is the bigger the better. They should always be framed, untinted and the silvering should be in good condition, If the mirroring is tarnished, wherever you hang it, it will bring in tarnished energy. If you hang it in the wealth area, it will bring in corrupt finances, in the relationship area, tainted relationships. Mirrors should not be used if they are damaged or cracked.

Mirrors can create the illusion of space, so if you have an L-shaped house with a missing area of the bagua hang a mirror on either of the two walls that border the missing area. You can then draw more energy into those areas.

Are you familiar with the old wives' tale that if you break your reflection in a mirror it means seven years of bad luck? Over time the expression has become altered. Originally it referred to the breaking of your reflection in any shiny material so if you threw a stone into a still pond and broke your reflection while you were gazing at it, it would mean seven years of bad luck. When you hang mirror tiles on your wall you are installing a permanent broken reflection of yourself. When you have large mirrors butted up against each other (like the ones you see in a gym), you are creating the same situation. If you have such a mirror scheme in your house, next time you get the opportunity, stand in front of it, look at your broken reflection and see how you feel. Look, too, at the reflection of one of your loved ones in the mirror and when you see their image all 'cut up' you will find that your heart beats a little faster. Your subconscious mind thinks that you have been cut into pieces and this has the result of damaging your health.

A bagua mirror is one of the most powerful cures

available. It is small and round and set inside an octagonal frame – a very powerful shape – and has the I Ching symbols inscribed around it, which act like runes. It is usually red, gold and green: a carefully chosen strong colour combination. Bruce Lee was living in a house in Hong Kong which had bad feng shui, and he hung a bagua mirror to deflect the shas. But during a fierce storm it fell off, leaving him without protection and he died.

There are many tales of the mirror wars of old China. During this time nearly every family had at least one bagua mirror in each window to deflect the sha coming from their neighbours. The result was that these shas were being bounced around in such a manner that they were creating accidents. Finally, magistrates legislated that each household was only allowed two bagua mirrors. Each house was searched for mirrors and the extra ones were confiscated and as far as I know that law remains in force today. The Chinese found their way around it by hanging or painting HUGE bagua mirrors that would fill the whole of the window on the wall opposite the front door.

It is regarded as bad feng shui if you live near a graveyard, hospital, mental asylum and such like. In hospitals and the like, there are very strong feelings of bitterness, grieving, sickness or anger and these emotional energies can pass through glass and walls, gradually building up and enveloping the houses nearby and influencing the occupants. To prevent spirit and malignant chi from entering your house, hang bagua mirrors.

Shiny objects also act as mirrors. Do any of you

remember 'witch balls'? They are like huge Christmas tree baubles and they are said to keep witches away, but what they actually do is deflect shas. The twentieth-century equivalent is the mayan ball – a 20mm (¾in) diameter, light-weight, shiny ball. I always wear one as a pendant over the heart area when I am teaching. It is impossible to keep everyone happy, as some people will want me to take more questions and others will want me to go faster. By wearing a mayan ball it deflects a lot of the negativity and gives some protection against psychological attack. If you have a difficult meeting, you are going on a long journey, or if you have moved in a direction which has upset your chi, leaving you prone to accidents, you can wear one to protect you.

Using mirrors as cures

- Whatever you reflect in a mirror, you draw into your home, so be aware of the image. If it is a view of nature and water, this is usually favourable but if it is a view of a police station or electrical pylons, this would not be auspicious. Mirrors should be hung flat against the wall, and you should be able to see all of your head and a decent space above and to the sides, so that you can 'see' your aura. If you can't, you will feel cramped and claustrophobic.

Bagua mirrors are the most powerful cure available. Hanging one so that it shines towards any threatening element will protect you and your family.

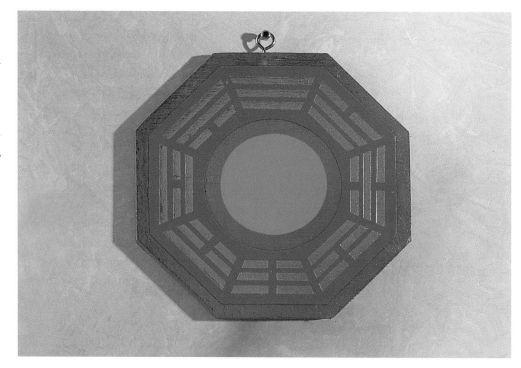

- Mirrors that are hung directly opposite each other can create an unstable environment as they bounce energy backwards and forwards too rapidly, making the residents feel uncomfortable. However, in certain situations you can use this to good effect – see Dining rooms, pages 56-61 and Bathrooms, pages 82-7.

- Mirrors can also be used to double the energy of something, so they are frequently used to reflect tills or fish tanks – this doubles the amount of money energy.

- Don't use convex mirrors to reflect your image, but to bring in more energy. They bounce energy in all directions, expanding it and making 'big' things happen quickly. Convex mirrors are beneficial in basements.

- Concave mirrors reduce the amount of energy, so they can be used to slow down energy or to diminish a negative sha.

- If you hang a mayan ball on a length of red ribbon from the reversing mirror of your car it can deflect accidents. I have many case studies where I have advised people who have moved in a direction which means accident to hang them from the reversing mirror of their car. After a period of time, some of them have telephoned to complain that it has pulled the mirror off the windscreen. The mayan ball itself weighs very little, so it is not heavy enough to pull off the mirror.

What will have happened was that the vibration of the accident had been deflected with a force that pulled the mirror off the windscreen. One gentleman who had a new car found that the mayan ball pulled the mirror off twice and the third time it pulled the mirror off and cracked the windscreen. From this we can deduce that it had deflected a serious accident. All my loved ones have them hanging from their mirrors, just in case.

The second cure: crystals

Crystals have a powerful capacity to activate chi as they fill a room with a rainbow of prisms. They have a long history. Healers would often inset them into their staffs to strengthen their charms and medicine and Kings and Queens of the world would inset them into their crowns so that they would be the centre of attention and energy would be drawn towards them.

Diamonds are the strongest and most effective form of crystal. If you were to hang a beautiful, large, flawless, sparkling faceted diamond in your window, the energy would be enormous. In fact, just picturing such a diamond can change your energy. Unfortunately, it is beyond the financial reach of most of us.

The crystals we use in feng shui are clear, faceted, and usually spherical. They have the ability to absorb chi and intensify it. They prevent energy from becoming stagnant in an area by sending out a myriad of colourful prisms that dapple the room and fill it with moving sun energy.

The first thing you should do with your crystal is to cleanse it. This involves running it under the cold tap and mentally cleansing it. To do this, just picture all the energetic dirt and grime being rinsed away while you wash off the physical dust. There are many different techniques of cleansing, but I find this is the quickest and simplest, and in this day and age when everyone is in such a hurry, the easiest technique is more likely to be practised regularly.

Next you should stand with your feet squarely on the ground and hold the crystal between your thumb and index finger and 'ask it to come to your heart'. Then slowly bring the crystal to your heart and think of what you want to use the crystal for. If it is going to be hung in the relationship area, fill your heart with the love you feel for your family, your friends, the birds and the plants. When you feel a connection (which may happen in seconds or it may take ten minutes), hang up the crystal and as the sun shines through it, it will bring in energy that is coloured with that emotion. It takes approximately three months for all the energy to pour out of the crystal so repeat this process every few months.

If you are going to hang a crystal in the wealth area, bring it to your heart and picture something like, walking through a golden forest of money trees during autumn. Imagine all the leaves are notes of a large denomination, with clusters of sparkling gold coins representing the fruit. Many have dropped onto the ground and you are wading through a carpet of money. Picture all the things you are going to do with the money: that new car, holiday, new house, until you feel a connection, then hang it in the window of the wealth area. You need to repeat this procedure every three months as the energy gradually leaks out and will need re-energising.

Normally you would hang a spherical faceted crystal in a window, close to the glass from a length of silver thread. If you are using a crystal in a dark area, then stand it on a piece of mirror. They can be used in any of the areas of the bagua to bring in some refreshing energy.

Healing crystals like amethyst, rose quartz and

such like need to be used with care, as they are medicine and they influence different organs of the body. If you take medicine every day it can make you poorly. These crystals will change the vibration of a room. They have an

Crystals can bring more energy into an area as they activate chi through their many prisms.

extraordinary habit of multiplying, so be careful not to have too many because they can make you dreamy, headachy and less well grounded.

The third cure: light

Light is energy, and the sun is the biggest light and has the greatest power to stimulate life. All living things, from moths to people, get drawn towards light, whether that light comes in the shape of fireworks, the Blackpool illuminations, or a street light. The level of lighting affects people's moods and therefore the sort of energy that they are sending off and filling the room with. You can use light in any area of the bagua to your advantage.

Some time ago I went to visit a couple who lived in a house which had been designed and built in the seventies and in the hall the lighting was inset into the wall, about 15 cm (6 in) off the ground and hidden behind rectangular, opaque, plastic panels. As I walked around the house I found myself starting to double over as I bent towards the light. When they changed the light to up-lights they started to 'walk tall' again and there is now a much brighter, happier atmosphere in the house as up-lights lift the chi. They are particularly useful in basements but I prefer to use them everywhere.

Candles

Candles emit a wonderful light and the energy they give off is very gathering. You will find that when you light a fire, people will gather round, and when you put it out, they will start to disperse. A candle is especially helpful in the relationship, knowledge and health areas. In a hallway, it is probably more practical to burn an aromatherapy burner than a naked candle to introduce the fire element.

Fluorescent tube lighting

Fluorescent tube lighting seems to vibrate at a particular frequency that is not beneficial for health. It seems to create more headaches than any other kind of light.

Halogen lighting

Halogen lighting has all the colours of the spectrum except infra red and ultra violet so it can combat seasonal affective disorder, to a degree.

Using light as a cure

- Down-lights bring the light down. If you live in a skyscraper or a tower block, down-lights can help to keep you more grounded. Central lights keep the energy in the centre of the room.

- When there is a missing area in a house, light can be used to bring that area of the bagua back into the house. Situate an outside light in the missing segment so that it fills the area with energy and make sure you switch this light on every evening, just as you would the indoor lighting.

- Another of my clients was finding that her children kept forgetting to take off their wellington boots before they came into the house from the garden. I suggested that she put a bright light on their indoor shoes just inside the front door and they started to remember more frequently.

- I hate doing my accounts so I ask my secretary to put my cheque books and statements on the desk once a month with a bright light shining on them and then it becomes very difficult for me to ignore them. Light draws all living things.

The fourth cure: sound

Abrasive sounds, like squeaking doors, car alarms or other people's music can create discordant chi that irritates the nervous system. Likewise, a noisy road or railway can disturb the energy. The sound waves from a bell or a wind chime vibrate the air and influence the chi. To help overcome this, hang a small metal wind chime (a big wind chime can damage your liver) with five hanging bars just above the front door inside the house so that every time the front door is opened it just touches the clapper at the bottom, causing it to chime. This vibrates and cleanses the atmosphere and absorbs any unhealthy earth shas that may occasionally (depending on the configuration of the planets) come in through your front door bringing sickness. When you have a wind chime here, sickness will tend to come into the house, perhaps in the shape of a cold, but it should be gone again in a much shorter period of time than you would usually expect.

Using sound as a cure

- Metal wind chimes should never be hung outside unless you have a very large plot of land or they will attract negative energy. Wooden ones are much more auspicious outside.

Candles have a gathering influence and are excellent for anywhere in the home where you like to sit and talk.

Wind chimes hung above the front door cleanse the atmosphere and dispel sickness.

- A wind chime placed in the ancestor area can occasionally help smooth family arguments. The wind chime reduces the amount of charged energy without eliminating it completely.

- A simple cure is to install an indoor bubbling water fountain which can make peace between the silence and the background noise but they do not neutralise the influences of the sound waves. These sound vibrations can stress the nervous system.

- Firecrackers are used by some feng shui consultants to frighten away spirits or to cleanse a house. The loud reports send vibrations through the atmosphere to, clean it.

The fifth cure: colour

Colour is one of the most vibrant and exciting cures, for with one splash of colour you can change the whole atmosphere of a room or garden. Colours clearly carry a vibration – if you paint a cold room blue, it will feel colder. But if you paint it yellow, it will feel warmer.

During each Chinese dynasty, a royal colour was chosen by a feng shui master, brown for the Sung dynasty, green for the Ming dynasty and yellow for the Ch'ing dynasty. The colour was selected by using the four pillars and the nine stars of destiny belonging the Emperor. He led the whole country, so if his energy levels were balanced and high, he could guide with wisdom and foresight. If his energy was off-balance, the whole country's would be. The colours of the Forbidden City in the heart of Beijing have followed feng shui principles by painting the walls red and the roofs yellow.

Depending on our date of birth, different colours will support us and give us more energy and others will drain us. How do you feel when you are dressed all in red? Does it make you shine, feel more vibrant and give you an added energy, or does it make you feel too conspicuous, and you therefore behave in a defensive way because you are feeling vulnerable? Likewise, if a person sees someone else dressed all in red it has a certain effect upon the senses, whereas if that person is dressed in blue a completely different emotion is stirred (see overleaf).

Different combinations of colour create extraordinary effects. Stripes can create arguments and confusion. Different colour combinations in different areas can influence your health. Let's have a look at the different attributes of colour in more depth.

115

Black is a powerful colour and it represents money, so use it sparingly, a little goes a long way. Black gives power. When used with pink it gives one social power, when with yellow, it gives intellectual power. Black is the colour that absorbs the most. When people start wearing black excessively they are usually in need of attention. So if your children suddenly express a desire to paint their room black they are feeling a bit insecure. Black represents the water element. This is a good colour to use in the career, wealth and ancestor areas.

Blue represents spiritualism, thoughtfulness, consideration and care. Blue is associated with faith, constancy and fidelity. When you need faith, think of royal blue. The colour is cooling and calming and it is generally the colour of an introvert. Businesses that use blue are adopting an identity of trustworthiness, reliability and honesty. This colour is of the water element and it is good to use it in the wealth, ancestor and career areas.

Brown is from the earth and, occasionally, the wood element. Light brown was the colour of mourning cards in China as it represents a time of keeping still. Those people who use brown in large amounts tend to be reliable, steady, stable, practical and down-to-earth. It is a good colour to use if you are a dreamer and a bit scattered, but if you are a slow and steady worker, this colour will turn you into a plodder and cause stagnation. Brown is an excellent colour to use in the knowledge, relationship, helpful people and children areas.

Green acts as a balance to our whole system, it represents balance, harmony and peace. When mixed with red, it is the colour of growth, and promotes healing and tranquillity. It can also encourage travel and jealousy. This is often the colour selected by business people because it is the colour of giving and receiving. When it is from plants, it reflects peace and harmony and will ease troubled minds. It is a colour that is linked to our heart centre and when we think green it attracts whatever we need. Too much green creates a static condition because it alleviates all stress and we all need a little stress to evolve. There is a shade of green known as 'hospital green' that is not a good colour to have around if you have a degenerative disease because it resonates with decay and will weaken health further. Green is from the tree element and it is good to use this colour in the wealth, ancestor and fame areas.

Grey is the colour the person who appears to be a conformist but is not really. It is also the colour of self-denial, and associated with fear and depression – on a grey day, life is not very good. If you are a fearful person, you should not use grey. The colour is associated with the water element. It can be used near the front door, in the career area, helpful people and children areas.

Orange is the colour of someone who tends to follow the crowd. It is a social colour and leads people into more social activities, and it is a creative colour, that represents joy, togetherness, constructive mental and physical energy. It is also the colour of the exhibitionist. If you are married and you use a lot of peach, you can attract too much energy into your relationships. The colour is from the fire or the earth element, depending on the shade. It is appropriate to use this colour in the relationship, knowledge, health, helpful people and children areas.

Pink is healing and represents love and romance. If you are feeling angry, think of pink and your anger will evaporate. Pink is a healing colour, it is warming, soothing and it raises our vibration so it is a very healthy colour to have around you. It also represents joy, happiness and especially romance. It belongs to the fire and the earth elements, depending on the shade, and it is good to use in the relationship and knowledge areas.

Purple is often considered by the Chinese to be more auspicious than red; they have a saying that 'it is so red, it is purple'. The colour belongs to the philosopher, the dreamer, the author and visionary. It is often associated with high ideals, loyalty, truth, love and suffering. It is the colour that was adopted by the church and is associated with the martyr because it can impel the wearer to sacrifice themselves for their ideals. Purple is the colour of the great orator. If someone has purple chi, it means high nobility, indicating that someone is a powerful, rich and fortunate individual. It is also the colour used as a seal by the very highest authorities. Purple belongs to the fire element and it is appropriate to use this colour in the relationship, knowledge and fame areas.

Red the colour of life, is the most auspicious colour of all. It relates to growth, happiness, joy, passion and virtue. If you lack courage, picture lots of red. Red is the great energiser, representing love – deep, passionate, love.

Chinese brides wear red because it is regarded as a lucky, happy, erotic colour. It also is a highly emotional colour. It you are over-emotional or hyperactive, it is not a good colour for you to have around in great quantities. Red, like black, has a very strong energy and works best in small amounts. In China, the expression 'he has a red heart' means he is without guile. Red is believed to keep away evil forces. It is of the fire element and it is appropriate to use accents of it in the relationship, knowledge and fame areas – never use too much.

White is the colour of mourning in China so it is not
used very frequently. The West regards white as the colour of purity, innocence, naivity, gullibility, and openness. If you have too much white in your home it can make it harder for you to have clear opinions, because it opens up too many possibilities. If you have too much white and lots of mirrors, your lungs can be damaged. White is from the metal element and it is appropriate to use it in the children area, helpful friends and career.

Yellow is the colour of the fabric that the dead are
buried in in China. It is the colour of control, and was therefore selected as the eternal national colour of China and it was reserved solely for the use of the Emperor and his descendants. Yellow is a very gathering colour, it stimulates mental energy and represents wisdom. The yellow ray helps our horizons to expand and it is a good colour for the elderly who may have become a little narrow-minded because it helps life to become more exciting and fun. Yellow also represents patience and tolerance. The colour is from the earth element and it is appropriate to use in the relationship, knowledge, helpful people and children areas.

Using colour as a cure
- If I want to do some brainstorming, I make sure I have splashes of strong colours around me, maybe in the shape of flowers or cushions, or even a piece of tinsel to inspire mental activity. If the colours surrounding you are dull and flat, it is much more difficult to be creative.

- Dark-coloured ceilings are not recommended as they create stagnant, blocked energy, and can shrink your energy field.

- If you want to attract a passionate relationship into your life, wear red and black. If you would like an

intellectual relationship, then wear yellow and black. When you are looking for love, wear pink and black. But if what you want is an adventurous, outdoor relationship, then wear green and black. If you are hoping for a spiritual relationship, then wear purple and black; and if you want to be slightly taken advantage of, wear white. If you are looking for an old-fashioned man or woman and a sensible, steady relationship, you should wear blue. You only need a splash of each colour. If you are a man, you could wear a red tie, say, or if you are a woman you could wear a red ribbon or a red brooch.

The sixth cure: heavy objects

Solid, heavy objects have a yang chi and they influence energy to move downwards. If you put a heavy, dense object near you, it will have a grounding influence. If you are using icons of faith like statues of Buddha or of Jesus, they should always be placed above ground level, and treated with respect. Heavy objects create stillness in an area and often the energy in a garden can move too fast. So statues are very

Red is a very auspicious colour – indeed, it is the colour of life.

beneficial in this area as long as they blend harmoniously with the landscape.

Salt is one of the most dense yang substances in the world and it can be used to absorb spirit energy and create a more stable atmosphere. If you use salt, it should be placed in a small metal or pottery bowl, sited in the knowledge area or near your front door and changed every three weeks.

Using heavy objects as a cure

● If you sleep in a room that is above an unoccupied space, like a garage, installing a heavy stone or concrete statue will help to ground your energy and make you feel more secure.

● If you have started a new job and you are feeling a little unsure of yourself, siting a statue or a heavy stone near the front door will ground the energy a little.

● If your relationships are going through an unstable phase, then put a pair of stone statues in the relationship area of the house to make it more steady.

● Metal – especially iron – alters the flow of the magnetic field, so objects of this material can be placed in the helpful people, career or the children area. This might be in the form of a clock or a metal sculpture.

● The areas of health and knowledge are associated with earth and they don't like water. If you have water in these areas you can place a metal object here and it will make peace between the conflicting elements of earth and water.

The seventh cure: animals

A healthy loving pet has a tremendously positive influence on your life. They surround you with the vibration of love. Statues and pictures of animals can also have a powerful influence on the atmosphere. Conversely, an unhappy, sick or fierce animal has a negative influence in a house. That doesn't, for a minute, mean get rid of your old, sick pet that you've had for twenty years, it just means you have to balance the energy with more healthy living things around you.

If you have a pet that is naturally sociable, don't keep it on its own, get it a mate. If you have an animal that was born

wild in a small cage, make sure it was born into captivity and is happy in a little cage or it will feel unhappy and send out a negative energy.

Every area of the bagua benefits from the energy of a healthy living animal. I once gave a consultation to a family who had a little boy who had a hamster. He loved it so much that every night he moved the cage close to his bed so it wouldn't be lonely. But for most of the time it lived in his relationship area and he had many friends. After about a year he moved it into the wealth area of his room and he immediately got a pay rise in his pocket money.

Birds in the garden are a very good omen and they activate the chi, bringing more energy into your plot. Doves in ancient times used to have whistles tied on to their tail feathers so that they would make a beautiful sound when they flew through the air. They are associated with the element of earth.

Butterflies should be encouraged into the garden, even if it is at the cost of a few leaves, they are a sign that there are few pesticides in the area and can be used as an indication of the condition of the land. They are associated with joy, charm and summer, and the element of fire.

Cats are credited with being able to ward off harmful spirits. It is very unlucky for a cat to leave you or be stolen. The cat belongs to the wood element, so bedding should be blue, black or green.

Chickens and cockerels together symbolise the pleasures of rural life. Chickens are courageous birds, they will defend their families to the end, and they are always scratching to find grain for their chicks. They are a symbol of life, warmth and benevolence. The cockerel belongs to the metal element.

Crickets in your garden are an auspicious sign. They are regarded as a symbol of immortality and resurrection. Wealthy Chinese descendants used to have a cricket carved out of a piece of jade and popped into the mouth of the deceased loved one to ensure eternal life happiness and the vigour of youth. The cricket belongs to the wood element.

Deer are an emblem of longevity as the deer is the animal that is supposed to have eaten the sacred fungus of immortality. If one wanders into your garden and eats all

Two courting doves are symbolic of peace and love.

your favourite flowers, take solace in the transcendental meaning, it is a sign that you will get a long-lasting promotion. The deer belongs to the wood element.

Dogs

add a wonderful energy of companionship, support and love to a house. The dog belongs to the earth element so their bedding should be brown, yellow, terracotta, burgundy or red. If a dog comes and finds you, it is an excellent omen for all the family.

Dragons

are the celestial animal. The dragon is king of all the aquatic beasts in the world. There are three species of dragon: the lung, the strongest which lives in the skies; the li, which is hornless and lives in the sea, and the chiao which lives in marshland and mountains. The dragon is regarded as a divine animal that can grant any wish and exert any punishment. If you can keep a statue or picture of a small green dragon in the ancestor area of your house it will look after all the residents. The dragon is an earth element with hidden water.

Elephants

are protective. The elephant is said to be the bearer of a wish generating gem, and it is a symbol of strength, wisdom and prudence. If you have a stone statue of an elephant and a pregnant lady places a pebble or a stone (depending on the size of your elephant), on top of him, it is said that he will ensure a safe, easy delivery and he will endure some of the pain of childbirth. Keeping an effigy of an elephant near a till will help profits to remain steady and help you to spend the money wisely. The elephant is associated with the metal element.

Fish

represent money, abundance and marital happiness and the element of water. They are best situated in the wealth area or near the entrance to a building. Gold-coloured cold water fish are the best sort to have in the West because they are the strongest. The fish with the strongest chi is the carp; it jumps out of water and it will probably be the next fish to evolve into a land form animal. If you add one carp to a tank of goldfish you will see that all the fish become much more active. An aquarium of gold-coloured

119

fish with a bubbling oxygenating pump stimulates very healthy chi. The best number of fish to have is nine: eight goldfish and one black fish; the black one will protect the family's health to a higher degree than the gold ones. Whenever a fish dies for no apparent reason it should be replaced straight away.

Your fish must be happy and healthy at all times. You need to have an oxygenator, a filter, a light, and a big enough tank for them to be happy. When the fish outgrow the tank, take them back to the pet shop or release them in your own or a neighbour's pond. A stressed animal sends out a stressed vibration.

I have experimented extensively with fish tanks and reached the conclusion that I will not live in a house without a tank. They have an extraordinarily positive influence on your finances. Placing a fish tank in the career area, can bring you money through your work. Fish tanks in the children area means your children may receive a scholarship, in the south they can mean rank or promotion, and in the knowledge area you can get money from selling your ideas or inventions. And on top of all that, they protect your health. What more could you want from a humble fish?

Whatever is happening in your life is somehow echoed in the fish tank, so if your fish start to eat each other, it is an indication of too much stress; if they become sickly and diseased, it is an indication of a sick energy around you. If they breed, it is a sign that lots of new projects are starting in your life. If they swim very fast around the tank or if they become slow and sleepy, it is an indication of what is happening in your life. It is very sad when they die, but if you have remembered to feed them, kept the tank clean and the pump in good working order and they die for no apparent reason, they have often absorbed a serious negative sha that you would have otherwise absorbed.

Foxes

are associated with supernatural things. Chinese people try to keep on good terms with foxes by leaving them offerings of incense and meat. In fact, many wealthy people credit their good fortune to the worship of this animal. When people commit suicide, it is said that they have to roam the earth until the time when they were supposed to die and during this time they live in the energy field of the fox. If you help the spirit living in the energy field of the fox it can also help you; if you harm it by harming the fox, the spirit can bring you bad luck. The fox is associated with the fire element.

Hares

in the form of pictures introduce a spiritual element into the home as they are said to get their energy from gazing at the moon. If you ever see one in your garden, it is a very auspicious sign as you will be blessed with luck, spiritual awareness and longevity from the gods. It is a wood element animal.

Horses

are regarded as fire element animals. They are an emblem of speed, quick wits and perseverance and bring these attributes to your household. By hanging up a horse shoe, tack or pictures or statues of horses, this positive energy will be activated.

Lions

guard the entrance to houses and temples. They used to be called the 'Dog of Fo' and are now known as Fu Dogs. They scare away demons and bad people and are a symbol of valour and majesty. The lion is not as strong as the tiger, so if a building nearby is threatening your house and they have lions outside, then you would need to site tigers to make all the sha disappear. The lion belongs to the small metal element.

Oxen

represent a time of plenty and an abundant season. They are emblems of spring so it is good to have a picture of an ox in the east northeast corner of your house. The ox belongs to the earth element.

Phoenixes

are said to appear only during times of peace and prosperity. It is the second celestial creature. It is the king of all the birds and it is very good to have a carving or picture of one at the front of your house. If you cannot find a phoenix, a red bird will do. The phoenix belongs to the fire element.

Rabbits

represent warmth, happy relationships and love and it is auspicious to keep this image in the relationship area. The rabbit belongs to the wood element.

Rats or mice

are a symbol of prosperity and an industrious nature because of their ability to find and acquire abundant food supplies. They belongs to the water element and a statue of a rat or a mouse can be placed in the north of the house.

Sheep or goats

are a symbol of a retired life of ease and filial respect (when a lamb feeds, it kneels down) so if you live in the country and have fields of sheep around, this is the sort of energy that the land will be tinged with. The sheep belongs to the earth element.

Swallows
making a nest in the roof of your house are a sign that success is just around the corner.

Tigers
are extremely dangerous and are supposed to live to an age of a thousand and then turn white. They represent the West while the green dragon represents the East and there is an expression that says if the white tiger gets too strong the dragon cannot control him and he will devour the occupants of the house. The tiger belongs to the metal element.

The tiger is another protector, he can scare away demons. In China, he is known as the king of beasts, and lord of all the land animals, and his effigy is regarded as a powerful talisman. He represents the masculine energy and symbolises military strength. Keep a sculpture of a tiger in the children area of your home to protect your children.

Tortoises
are the fourth celestial creature and it is considered auspicious to keep a statue of one at the back of the house looking out towards the garden or the street. It belongs to the earth element.

Unicorns
are fabulous mythical creatures of good fortune, a symbol of longevity, riches, joy, grandeur, kindness, wisdom, and powerful, happy children. It is very good to have a picture or statue of a unicorn in the children area of the house because it enhances the likelihood of having successful wise children.

The eighth cure: plants

Imagine a world outside without plants. It wouldn't be very pleasant. Your home is a microcosm of the macrocosm and it can only benefit from plants. Today we live in such an artificial environment, with synthetic wall and floor coverings, lots of electrical activity, surrounded by a concrete jungle and non-stop traffic, so plants are invaluable. They represent growth and peace of mind. If a plant cannot live in a room, then nor can a person. If your plants keep dying, it is an indication that you are not looking after your health properly. Green, healthy, verdant plants in the area around

your building are a sign of excellent, healthy chi. Conversely, bare, brown patches are a sign of sickness and separation.

Plants are very useful everywhere in the house. You may have to make some minor modifications like tying a red ribbon around the plant pot in the relationship area, but generally you can position them liberally all over the house. Small plants can represent clutter, so big ones are preferred. Plants are used to mask sharp corners, absorb electrical vibrations and to slow down energy.

Plants with sharply pointed leaves, like a yucca, cacti or pineapple, have been receiving a lot of bad press recently. This is because they have a negative influence in a small space; they need a large expanse of desert to absorb the cutting chi they send out from their spiky leaves. If you tap the back of your hand against a pineapple plant, you will irritate the skin. They are therefore particularly bad if placed too near a seat, bed or workplace. If you have lots of spiky plants near your front door, they will discourage visitors; in the relationship area they will discourage romance.

Money plants, or jade plants, however, are very auspicious as they strengthen your finances and your luck. Your own chi becomes interlinked with the plants so beware, because if they die or sicken – you can expect to have a problem with your money luck.

Fresh flowers, are a wonderful gift, energetically many times more valuable than chocolates. Cut flowers send out more energy than plants and they absorb stress and anger. I have three beautiful bunches of carnations on my desk at the moment; one on either side of my computer, and one on the far right-hand corner. Not only do they absorb electrical pollution but the bright colours also inspire me. It is very beneficial to keep red or pink flowers in the relationship area and also in the hall near the front door.

Azaleas and rhododendrons
are sometimes called 'the goat stupefying flower'. This is because they are narcotic and goats have been known to sample them with interesting results. These beautiful plants are said to strengthen everybody's health, as they absorb some of the chi that creates rheumatism, paralysis, and toothache.

Bamboo
is said to have mystical qualities of longevity. It can be made into flutes which are suspended from beams to negate the influences of division; they should be hung in pairs to form the beginning of a bagua shape with red ribbon tied round them.

Bonsai trees have all the energy of a fully-grown tree. They can strengthen your health and your finances, so place them in the fame, ancestor or wealth area.

Cherry is a popular emblem of the fairer sex. If you plant one at the birth of a baby girl it is said that it will strengthen her health and make her happy and wise.

Chrysanthemums are symbols of joviality, bringing laughter and joy to the grower. They have beautiful Chinese names like 'heaven full of stars' or 'drunk with wine made from the peaches of the immortals'. The chrysanthemum is said to bring a life of laughter, ease and retirement to the grower and his household.

Conifers or pine trees signify longevity, and it is particularly auspicious to plant one for a boy at his birth. To border your home with evergreen hedges will promote longevity. Hedges that lose their leaves represent poor health.

Jasmine is known as the plant of friendship, if you have ever smelled one on a warm and balmy evening and paused to enjoy the fragrance which smells sweeter in the evening, you will appreciate this apt title.

Lilies are very auspicious for everyone. They are reputed to be the most sacred and important and every single part of the plant is used for something. They are emblems of purity and perfection, classed as one of the eight treasures, and used extensively in carpet designs to bring summer and fruitfulness to a house.

Magnolias are known to the Chinese as the Secretly Smiling Flower. The plant is said to make a woman more sweet and beautiful. This probably relates to its medicinal uses.

Narcissi are known as the Water Fairy. They are grown from bulbs and forced into blossom exactly at the new year to bring good fortune for the next twelve months.

Pear trees should be planted in government or large corporate buildings because they bring with them the influence of impartial justice, wisdom and benevolent administration. They also bring longevity.

Peonies are known as the Flower of Riches and Honour and they strengthen the male energy. One species is known as 'Male Vermilion'. It is an emblem of love and affection and is said to strengthen the man's heart, blood disorders and congestion if planted in the north-west quadrant of the garden. It is regarded as an omen of good fortune if it becomes full of beautiful flowers and green leaves. On the other hand, if a peony suddenly fades, it foreshadows poverty or disaster in the family of the owner.

Plum is the symbol of winter and long life. So a plum tree will bring the chi that helps to create a long life and a natural death.

Roses have the transcendental meaning of 'short lived relationships', but only if they are planted near a path or doorway.

The ninth cure: symbols

If everyday all you see around you is dark and barren scenery it will make you sad. If you see flowers and wildlife, it will make you feel happy and cheerful. We are very susceptible to whatever we have around us. Imagine if you hung a magnet saying 'kick the cook' on the fridge, and a five-year-old came to visit you, what do you think he would do when he read the magnet? Now, if you had a magnet saying 'arms are for hugging' or 'kiss the cook', what do you think he would do then? When we grow up, we don't change, our subconscious mind still helps us to make nearly all the decisions!

If you had an appointment to meet me and my name was Miss Ugly or Miss Cruel, what sort of opinions would you form about me before we met? But if my name was Miss Darling or Miss Kind, you would have another impression of me. It may be completely illogical, but nonetheless your first impression has far reaching influences.

In a similar way, whatever you see around you in your home is going to have an influence on your life. I can always tell what is going on in someone's house by looking at their pictures. If there are no pictures, then the person living there tends to be lonely and depressed. If there are lots of pictures, statuettes or lamps of single women or groups of women, that tells me that a single woman with lots of girlfriends lives there. If there are lots of pictures of Bob Marley and pictures of marijuana leaves, that tells me something else. Lots of pictures of water indicates someone who is still looking for their life path.

If you go and see a happy film, like *The Long Kiss Goodbye*, you will tend to come out feeling warm and friendly. But if you were to see *Reservoir Dogs*, the chances are you will end up feeling aggressive and assertive. If you were to wait in a room that was hung with drawn swords, spears, axes, knives and daggers it is going to make you feel a little bit 'hard'. But if you are waiting in a room that has two little kittens curled up and as you look at them, they start to purr, it is going to make you feel warm and soft (assuming you like cats!). Your aura therefore softens and you send out a warm energy that fills the room.

You need to be very attentive to the symbols you have around you. Your home is your castle, your sanctuary, it is where you go to recharge your batteries. So it needs to be a safe, warm and welcoming place. The easiest way to create that impression is by putting up pictures and symbols like 'home is where the heart is' or a family flying a kite in the park, or a couple sitting on a bench feeding the ducks. You need to look at the picture with your heart, not just your eyes, before you decide whether you like it sufficiently to hang in your home.

Money

has a powerful energy, but be careful, it is so strong that sometimes it can take over completely. If you make up a collage of real money and put it in your wealth area it can have a very healthy influence on your finances.

The first time money is minted, the printers are watching all those lovely notes and thinking 'Ooh, look at all that lovely money'. Then it will go into the vault and you will go to the bank and draw out some notes and as you take it in your hands, you think 'Ooh, look at all that lovely money'. You then might go to the clothes shop and buy yourself a blouse, and the shop keeper will take your fresh, crisp note and go to the greengrocers who will be very happy to receive it and he will put some of his energy into it, and so on. As the money passes from person to person, so it gradually collects more and more energy.

One of my friends and clients was a kind, intelligent and wealthy Canadian. He had a lovely, eloquent family but he had a rather poor relationship with them and ominously by the age of 51 he had suffered three heart attacks. We met for lunch and I remember talking to him and asking him why he didn't retire. He was a very successful oil developer, he had more money than he knew what to do with, he had more money than his wife and children knew what to do with. And I explained about the feng shui concept that money has its own energy and that when it is out of balance

it can take you over. He laughed and said he thought there might be something in it.

I offered to come and balance his home, to take away some of the money energy. But he definitely was not having any of that, although he did concede to take a year off. A couple of months later I heard that he had discovered another oil well, he was making a fortune and he was rushed off his feet. A month later he suffered another massive heart attack and he died.

So you see, money can be bad for your health and it is highly addictive. Have you ever smoked and tried to give up? It's even harder to give up or cut down on money than it is tobacco. But beware, there is a saying in China: more wealth, less health.

Symbols for each area

- In the entrance: it is symbolically very auspicious if one of the first things you see when you come into your house or office is three fish.

- In the fame area: keep your goals in this area, it might be a copy of a coveted cup or pictures of a car you want, or the cover of your book. Also position pictures or statues of animals like a cockerel, a phoenix, tortoise or a dragon here.

- In the relationship area: hang a picture of you and your partner taken when you were very happy together or pictures or statues of rabbits or a couple. In addition, keep a white vase with red or pink flowers here.

- In the wealth area: a collage of real money, statues or pictures of water, deer, nature or fish are very auspicious symbols.

- In the ancestor area: a photograph of your ancestors, a picture or statue of a green dragon.

- In the knowledge area: picture of a mountain, a moon-gazing hare, an elephant or a tortoise.

- In the helpful people area: pictures of angels, clouds (such as the photograph overleaf) and stars, and destinations you want to travel to.

- In the children area: a picture or statues of children, a tiger (a white tiger is especially lucky), a unicorn or a Buddha with children.

Put a picture like this in your benefactor area to improve the vibrations in this part of your home (see symbols on the previous page).

The tenth cure: revolving and moving things

These are windmills, mobiles, fans, silk banners, ribbons, weather vanes and revolving doors. The revolving motion circulates chi and can disperse malignant energy. If you have a dark, dank basement or cellar, putting a fan on for a few hours every now and then stops it becoming stagnant and sickly. If you have a missing area, putting some windmills in the garden will bring more energy to that area. If I were to say to you 'what's on your bedroom floor?', immediately, energetically, you have gone to your bedroom. As you do this, you take energy to that area. In the same way, when anyone sees movement in the missing area of your home, it draws their attention, which brings energy into that area and the movement stops chi from travelling too fast or too slowly.

Using moving things as a cure

● If you live in a tropical country and you have a beam across your bed you can hang a rotating fan above the bed from the beam and it will disperse the cutting chi.

● It is good to have a fan in the wealth area because this area likes movement.

The eleventh cure: transcendental cures

Professor Lin Yun, a feng shui teacher, always describes transcendental cures as working in the following way. If, for example, you are having problems with your relationships, you can try going to a marriage guidance counsellor, you could go on holiday together, or send each other flowers and it will probably work ten per cent. Or, you can try a transcendental cure, which may seem illogical, but we say it works 110 per cent because not only does it improve your relationships with your partner but also with everybody else in your life.

In ancient China, red paper scrolls were, and still are, used in pairs to protect the home. Red articles are believed to be able to keep away bad influences. The scrolls are symbolic of both thanksgiving and repentance. People used to smear the door posts and lintels with the blood of a sacrificial lamb (indeed, many different cultures did this, including the Jewish people) and in certain provinces in China, people still mix sheep's blood and plaster to colour the wooden door posts and window frames. It was believed that when you built a village or a house, you needed to cut down so many trees that the divas that lived in them became upset, so the sacrifice was made to appease the spirits. Centuries passed and paper was invented, so instead of blood, red paper or wood was used. As still more time passed, the red paper started to be inscribed with decorative motifs, and then with blessings.

Today, charms against evil spirits are often written in black or red ink on yellow paper. They are then pasted over a door, on a bed post, or sometimes they are burnt and the ashes are mingled with hot water and drunk at a specific time. For example, to dispel evil influences, a scroll of yellow paper with four characters on it would be hung from the highest eaves. This would always be done in association with the three secrets (see below) to reinforce the cure.

Many Chinese families or businesses keep the house where they made their fortunes. Even when they move to a more expensive and bigger house they still keep the little old one, perhaps as a future home for their children or they rent it out. I know many Chinese business men who have kept their original office where they made their fortune, even if it is in a very grotty area.

Some transcendental cures

To implement transcendental cures you need to use what is known as the three secrets:

1   A mudra, which is a hand gesture.
2   A mantra, which is a sort of prayer.
3   Visualisation, to imagine the result you want to reinforce the cure.

For a Feng Shui consultant to give transcendental cures he must be paid in a red envelope.

● For your health: if you are visiting a friend in hospital keep some orange peel in your pocket for the duration of the visit, then burn it in a fire to keep you strong and healthy.

● To create peace: beams can create arguments and sickness. Hang two bamboo flutes from red ribbon with the mouthpieces angled downwards and towards the corner of the room to absorb the negative charge.

● To strengthen health: spiral staircases are very bad for the health, especially if they are in the centre of the house. Thread green ribbon or cord through the banisters to make the influence much more favourable.

● For unemployment and depression: greet one new person for the next 27 days. Do not ask for anything or complain.

● For making money: get a china pig money box and put it under the bed. Put in a coin every day for 27 days and enforce with the three secrets every night as follows:

The mudra: cup your right hand palm up, then place your left hand palm down on top, and touch the thumbs together. Then raise your hands to chest level.

The mantra: Om Ma Knee Pad Me Ohm (recite nine times).

Visualise what you want as clearly as you can.

* For those who are depressed and stuck: move 27 things in your house that have not been moved for a long time everyday for the next nine days, while using the three secrets, as above.

Cleansing

Do you remember what I said at the beginning of the book about concepts from another culture being difficult to grasp? Well cleansing is probably the most difficult facet. But it is not a concept which was solely reserved for the Chinese people. Even today many people have house-warming parties and in Derham Groves' book *Feng Shui and Western Building Ceremonies* he tells about a house-warming party at his parents' house where a group of his parents' friends arrived banging saucepans with wooden spoons and throwing stones on the roof, to scare away evil spirits. This is a form of cleansing. If the method of cleansing given opposite and overleaf seems a bit overwhelming, you can simply explode some firecrackers in each room of your new home. But read the next few pages before you decide.

Everything needs cleansing sometimes, the dirty dishes after a meal, our clothes, we even meditate to cleanse ourselves of all the endless mind chatter. Meditating makes our minds resonate at a different vibration. Every culture has a different technique from chanting and dancing to breathing and praying, each one aimed at purifying our bodies and taking us to a new plane of thinking.

Over time, the atmosphere of the planet can absorb lots of different energies and the air becomes polluted or heavy with vibration. We divide the atmosphere into seven different levels beginning with the atmosphere you find in a cave, which is often dank and heavy so the chi can become stagnant and dirty very easily because there is no movement. The seventh is a mountain which is constantly being cleansed by the movement of the winds. Temples or sacred places have a high energy and they are often found on mountains. Another level is the polluted energy of an asylum or a prison. In these places, people send out a great deal of negative energy in the form of strong emotions like sadness, anger or depression and they also tend to be enclosed spaces where the vibrations build up because they cannot be dispersed easily by the natural elements of nature. Likewise, houses tend to be enclosed spaces where vibrations can build up, especially in the winter, when we keep everything sealed.

These vibrations stick to everything. Have you ever been to a medium who has taken something of yours like a ring and been able to tell you all sorts of things about yourself, that they shouldn't have known? The object absorbs some of your energy, and this is why people want to keep something that used to belong to a loved one who has passed on because it has the energy imprint of the owner.

Things that happen in buildings get absorbed by the walls, the floors, the furniture, ornaments, plants, even pets, and they are permanently recorded until cleansed. Any strong emotions that occur leave an energetic trace as people walk backwards and forwards leaving an imprint. Have you ever basked in the warm glow of a happy family home, or perhaps you have walked into a room after a quarrel and felt the tension? People say 'you could cut the air with a knife', which is very appropriate. If there is a room where arguments often occur, or a room where you always feel depressed, there can be an energy imprint left behind which you absorb whenever you go into the room.

Negative energy tends to build up and collect, particularly in the corners, like cobwebs. The North American Indian, Inuits and various tribes from all over the world would only live in round houses because they believed that evil collected in the corners. Even in the West, people don't like spooky dark corners, where things might be lurking. The vibration sticks to objects first, and the biggest build-up is found in the corners of the walls and ceilings. There is not so much on the floor because there is more movement which tends to 'dust' it away.

Old houses can collect centuries of vibrations so they are most satisfying to cleanse, because you can really notice the difference. I once went to a little old mews house in central London where the predecessor chi was so heavy that near the walls you could feel it like a cold, heavy mist and it took three bouts of space cleansing to remove it.

What you will need

Candles One or more: they always need to be white if they are being used for cleansing.

Incense sticks Set of three purifying incense sticks: these are about 30 cm (12 in) long and 12 mm (½ in) in diameter and are bought in sets of three. The best incense has mantras embossed in pink and dragons in gold, pink and green swirled around the incense and the smoke comes from the mouth of the dragon.

Incense holders Incense can be very messy, so always contain it in a vessel.

Basilica church incense This is the incense traditionally used in the church. It comes in little granules and you need to put them on top of a charcoal tablet and burn in a little incense pan which looks like a frying pan with a lid, which you can purchase from church shops.

Smudge stick The smudge stick originated in North America and it is made of herbs: sweet grass, sage and cedar are the most popular. When making up a smudge stick, you should always ask permission of the plant and thank it, and never pick the whole plant. Dry it and form a thick bundle tied together with a length of cotton thread.

Matches To light the candles, incense and smudge stick.

Holy water This is water that has been energised with mantras and prayers. The water is put into a bowl or a font, candles and incense are lit, a sacred bell is rung over the water, sometimes salt is added, and then for a long time, mantras and mudras are performed over the water.

When to cleanse?

It is very important to cleanse after there has been a death or an illness. The vibration left behind can be sickly, so wash all the bedding and the whole house. You might even decorate, then cleanse it thoroughly as is explained below.

Always cleanse a house when you move away. All your memories, the laughter, the tears that you have felt over the years are filling the house and if you leave without removing them, you will feel like you have left a bit of you behind.

Directly after you have moved into a house, emptied and decorated it, then cleanse it because whatever the previous occupant's energy was like, you don't really want to absorb it. It is much better to start afresh.

When to consider cleansing
- When the building is on a graveyard or ancient burial ground.
- When the house has been built on a battle field or a place where executions or mass killings took place.
- When the house, or the building that was on the

spot where your house is now, was a slaughter house, butcher's shop, funeral parlour, morgue, hospice, prison, asylum or hospital.
- When the building was vacated because of a bankruptcy.
- When a person died early or accidentally in the house.
- When someone has been murdered in the house.
- When there has been a robbery or a fire.
- If you consider the building has bad karma.

When to consider not cleansing
- If you are feeling nervous or frightened.
- After dusk.
- When you are having a period or have an open wound. Women who are menstruating are not allowed into temples because the blood attracts a negative energy so you can make the energy more dirty than it was before you started.
- When you are poorly or the energy you put into the house will be poorly.
- When you are pregnant.

Flowers   Red, yellow and white, one of each: the red flower represents happiness, love
and life; yellow represents laughter and joy and white represents healing and cleansing.

Bells   The ringing of bells is fancied everywhere in the world to banish demons and
spirits. The manner of ringing is different in each country. In a Buddhist document it
says, 'The sound of the bell procures relief and solace to the souls tormented in the
Buddhist hell. The undulatory vibrations, caused by the ringing of the bells, provokes to
madness the king of the demons, render him unconscious, blunt the sharp-edged blades
of the torturing tread-mill, and damp the ardour of the devouring flames of Hades.'
Liang-Pan ts'iu-yu-hoh

Mayan ball   I often wear a mayan ball around my neck over the heart area for
protection.

Drums   These can also be used to cleanse spaces; use them before you start with the
bells.

Using a smudge stick

To light a smudge stick, apply the flame until it burns brightly and then blow out the flame. Hold the smudge stick
in one hand and it will continue to smoke as you walk along the length of the wall. Blow the smoke in the direction
you want it to flow and in your other hand hold something to catch the ash. If you are smudging people, blow the
smoke gently but directly at the person. Do not hold the smudge stick too close to the person because it burns at a
high temperature. When the person has been surrounded by smoke, waft the air around them with a feather which
will cleans their aura further.

The cleansing procedure

1 Hoover, dust and clean the house. Ask everybody to
leave unless they are going to help you. Switch off the
television and stereo. Open a window. Energy can move
through walls but it moves more rapidly through windows.

2 Have a shower, or at least wash your hands, arms and
face. Then remove all your jewellery, watch and shoes.
These objects can absorb the mucky energy and you will
then have to cleanse them. And when you have your shoes
off you are receiving more of earth's energy. If it is cold,
keep your socks on.

3 Protect yourself. If you are feeling fearful, you should
not be cleansing the house. This is your subconscious
mind telling you that the house is too much for you to do.
Ask a friend to help you and then see how you feel. If you
still feel apprehensive, get a professional to cleanse it for you.

4 Light a white candle and one of the sticks of incense in
the centre of the house. The universal law is that you
always have to give before you receive, so offer up the candle
and the incense to your ancestors and guides and ask for
assistance and protection for you and everybody in the house.

I think it is wise to protect yourself the first few times you cleanse. One technique is to put yourself in a bubble of light (any colour that feels right except red) and surround the bubble of light with a thick crust of sea salt. The bubble is stronger than steel and surrounds your aura (which is roughly the extent of your outstretched arms). Try it now ... picture or feel the light ... that's it ... you are protected. You don't have to keep concentrating on the bubble to keep it there, your subconscious mind will keep it there until you don't need it anymore.

5 Now ask permission to cleanse the house. When you feel a 'smile in your heart' you know you have got that permission.

6 Light the other two sticks in the set of three and put one at the centre of each floor in an incense holder. If you only have one floor, put one stick near the front door and one at the back door. If you only have one front door, then put the third one near an open window at the other end of the house. Put the red, white and yellow flowers near the candle.

7 Take either a smudge stick or a little church incense holder with basilica incense in it and, starting at the front door, waft the incense along every wall, and in every corner, and while you are doing this, state your intention to clean the house. I sometimes make up a little rhyme saying something like I am cleaning the house, filling it with love and laughter. You need to finish where you started, at the front door, where you make a figure-of-eight pattern with the incense.

8 Now wash your hands, arms and face in cold water and then go back to the candle and thank your guides and ancestors for helping you and ask them to help with the next step.

9 Chant 'Om ma nee pad me omm' all the time as you walk around the house – this is a protective and enforcing mantra. To start the stagnant energy moving, go to the front door and then clap loudly three times in every corner of the house, and continue all around the house until you end up back at the front door. The first clap

should be quite low down, the next one a bit higher and the last one at the highest point you can reach.

10 Repeat step 8. Then either chanting the same mantra or singing a little rhyme about cleansing, take the loudest bell and tap it with a baton to make it ring loudly and don't let it stop vibrating (one continuous peal of sound) until you have gone around every corner and every room. Start at the front door and don't stop until you are back at the front door once again. Before you finish, move the bell in a figure-of-eight pattern until it has finished vibrating and the house is quiet.

11 Repeat step 10, but with a smaller, higher-pitched bell. Then repeat step 10 again, but with the smallest bell.

12 Wash your hands, arms and cheeks one more time in cold water and go back to the candle, thank your invisible assistants, ring each bell three times in the candle flame and mentally cleanse each one and mentally offer the ring of the bell to your helpers.

13 If you have any holy water, pour some into a clean bowl and dip the three flower heads in the water and shake them liberally in the room to disperse the water around the room paying special attention to corners and beds. If you have been wearing a mayan ball, cleanse this, too, by submerging it in the holy water and then leaving it to dry naturally.

14 Any water that is left pour on to the earth just outside the front and back doors. Wrap the flowers in tissue papers and dispose of them somewhere that nobody will touch them.

15 Cleanse yourself and your friend if they have been helping you with a smudge stick (see page 129).

16 When the house is finished, you will need to shield it. You can hang mayan balls or bagua mirrors at strategic points in the windows or above the door and mentally shield the building. To do this, first of all close your eyes and picture your house or flat, then raise your hand from the elbow up, and bring it down making a shh noise and visualise a shield of light coming down with the force and strength of a roller-type garage door all along one

To help cleanse your home you will need the help of three purifying incense sticks, a candle, and some red, yellow and white flowers.

of the outside walls of your home. Repeat as many times as necessary until you have gone all the way around the house and then roll a similar shield over the top and the bottom. I then spiral the whole lot in a rotating light and that's it — you've finished cleansing your home.

17 Now you need to cleanse you. So, within the next six hours, have a bath in water that contains at least one mug of salt for a minimum of ten minutes. Then have a shower in water that is as cool as you can bear and you will be clean once again.

Directionology

The earth is swathed in magnetic bands of energy (the Van Allen belts) and as a result there are many, many currents in the atmosphere and in the oceans. Some are governed by the moon, some by the poles, and some by gravity. For example, there is an especially powerful current in the sea flowing from the North pole to the equator. If we were to drop a sealed bottle with a message inside at the North pole, it would drift to the equator.

One of my teachers once told me this lovely story to explain the significance of the magnetic belts. Once upon a time, a very happy little fish was swimming around in the sea at the North pole. He couldn't see the water he was swimming in, in just the same way that we cannot see the air we are living in. One day, the little fish swam into the current, he didn't know he had gone into the current, so he didn't swim out of it. Every day he darted around, swimming first to the left and then to the right, swimming here and there, nibbling at seaweed and chatting to his friends, until one day he found himself at the equator. Now did he have free will? Yes and no, but he ended up in the warm seas thinking that he had consciously made all the decisions that led him to be there. If you cannot see a force, it does not mean it is not there. People will tell you that we have free minds and can do what we want, but this is not entirely true. Magnetic and cosmic fields have a significant and relentless influence on us.

Saturn is regarded as the central planet and moving towards or away from its position can have profound effects upon your life.

We all have our own in-built compass needle. At the heart of every blood cell in the human body is haemoglobin and at the centre of this is a trace of iron. If you put some iron filings on a piece of paper and put a magnet next to them you will see that they all move around and follow the magnetic pull. Similarly, the way that the energy emanating from the magnetic belts is moving around us determines how our internal compass is being influenced. It establishes how balanced we are in the energy field surrounding us. This influence will dictate whether our intuition is strong and giving us correct information, which will lead us to say and do the right thing at the right time, or whether we are inclined to accidents because our chi is off-balance.

Every time you travel on holiday for a long distance, or move house as little as 1 ½ miles, you are influenced by the Van Allen belts, which affects your energy. If you move more than 1 ½ miles and stay there for a minimum of three months, the resulting influence of moving into a new band of magnetic energy will last an average of three to fifteen years, or until you move again. The further you move, the more intense the influence. You will also be influenced if you travel a great distance to go on holiday or during a business trip, even if it is just for a short period of time. These distances and times are not cast in stone as these energies are not easily measured, so the distance and times given here are approximate.

Charlie Chaplin

Charlie Chaplin made a very auspicious move when in 1917 he moved west from Chicago to California. His career took off, he met Oona who he was in love with all his life, he found fame and fortune. If he had moved in 1918, this direction would not have been as auspicious.

Have you ever had the experience of going on holiday and really having the most wonderful time? And having had such a marvellous time you may have decided to go back the following year, but when you arrived you found you didn't really recover from jet lag for the whole time you were there? You kept losing things, you went to a business meeting, missed the nuance and lost the deal? These types of events would have been the result if you had moved in a direction which took your energy away.

If you move in a direction which makes your energy too strong, then you will probably experience lots of needless quarrels. Or you might meet somebody and ask her, quite casually, what she is doing and she will probably respond by telling you to 'mind your own business'. When you move in a direction which intensifies your chi too much, you will tend to come across too strongly for people to cope, and you can appear too intense. You might also experience accidents through being too impulsive, and generally find yourself getting irritable rather too quickly.

What happened to me

To write this book I decided to rent a cottage that was situated in a good direction for me to travel which meant I would receive more support, and stronger intuition. Unfortunately, I could not move in a good month because I had left it too late. But as the deadline for the book was fast looming I had to move in a bad month, and this is what happened to me while I was trying to write.

When I arrived, I promptly caught a cold. I had forgotten a disc that had all my course notes and research on it. And worst of all, my computer expired. I then spent the whole day speaking to two angels, otherwise known as computer aces Jason and Ian, who talked me through the problems and although we managed to revive the computer, I had lost one of my precious days.

The second day, my newly appointed temporary secretary who was going to look after the office for a month while I wrote the book and my wonderful PA, Katrina, took a well-earned holiday, telephoned to say she was poorly and could not do the job. This, of course, left me with some problems. I then took on a telephone answering service, but I forgot to ask my partner Rowland to divert the phone to them. A daily newspaper also telephoned on the same day to ask if I could do a trial page, as long as I could write the text within the next three hours – another day lost.

Despite that, as expected, I have had enormous support because I moved in the year's auspicious direction, enabling me to sort out everything very quickly. Moving in the wrong month means the negative influences generally only last for a short period of time, so I should be 'out of the woods' by now. The moral of the story is always move in the right direction at the right time. Make sure you are in harmony with the natural 'flow' of the universe, and then everything comes to you easily.

Finding good directions in which to move

Depending on which year you were born, a particular direction is auspicious to you. Below is a brief guide to some of the better directions for moving and their influences so that you can enhance your next house move. Wherever you have been sleeping for the past three months becomes the centre of the universe, and you take all your coordinates from this

The position of The Grand Duke and the Chinese animal year

Each year starts in accordance with the oriental calendar which is around the 4 or 5 February

Rat	2008	1996	1984	1972	1960	the rat is found in the north
Ox	2009	1997	1985	1973	1961	the ox is found in the north northeast
Tiger	2010	1998	1986	1974	1962	the tiger is found in the east northeast
Rabbit	2011	1999	1987	1975	1963	the rabbit is found in the west
Dragon	2012	2000	1988	1976	1964	the dragon is found in the east southeast
Snake	2013	2001	1989	1977	1965	the snake is found in the south southeast
Horse	2014	2002	1990	1978	1966	the horse is found in the south
Goat	2015	2003	1991	1979	1967	the goat is found in the south southwest
Monkey	2016	2004	1992	1980	1968	the monkey is in the west southwest
Rooster	2017	2005	1993	1981	1969	the rooster is found in the west
Dog	2018	2006	1994	1982	1970	the dog is found in the west northwest
Pig	2019	2007	1995	1983	1971	the pig is found in the north northwest

The Grand Duke correlates to Jupiter and is identified by the position of the Chinese animal signs and you should never move in the opposite direction to them. This means that in the year 2000, you should not move west northwest, even for a short holiday, because it is the year of the dragon and the dragon is found in the east southeast. If you do move away from him, you can expect a break-up or separation of relationships, or a dissolving of prosperous business transactions and negotiations.

Establishing the points of the compass

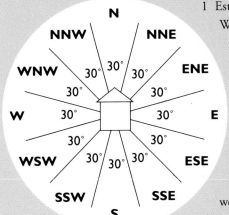

1 Establish where is north, east, south and west. We use magnetic north but it is quite close to true north so you can use a map, but don't go too near the boundaries. Most maps are orientated with north 'up' so this makes it easy to establish the four cardinal points.

2 North, east, south and west are found in a thirty-degree sector, fifteen degrees either side of magnetic north, east, south and west. East northeast, north northeast, west southwest, etc, etc, are also found in thirty-degree sectors.

point. I have also provided some past dates so that you can look back and see the results from previous house moves. This is only an introduction to the subject and there are many more directions that need to be avoided or emphasized than those listed below. For further reading, see the books outlined on page 139.

The Fives

Another direction you should avoid is towards or away from the planet Saturn, identified by the position of the five in the flying stars (for its position each year, see the table to the right). Moving towards or away from five can result in yet more difficulties.

Moving away from Saturn is called anken-satsu, which means dark sword killing symbolizing a sword coming from the shadows where you can't see it and don't expect it. If you travel in this direction, something unexpected can happen to you like an accident, robbery or losing something important. These things tend to happen suddenly.

If you move towards five, it is known as go-o-satsu, which roughly translated means yellow sword killing. The yellow represents the five itself (Saturn) and has the ability to create or destroy. If you move in this direction we say 'you start to eat yourself'. It can lead to gradual destruction of your health and you can become poorly. There can also be a break down of family relationships or business failure, but this process tends to happen slowly and gradually.

Saturn's annual position

Each year starts in accordance with the oriental calendar which is around the 4 or 5 February

In 1978, 1985, 1987, 1994,1996, 2003, 2005, 2012, 2014 and 2021 do not move northwest or southeast.

In 1979, 1984, 1988, 1993, 1997, 2002, 2006, 2011, 2015 and 2020 do not move west or east.

In 1980, 1983, 1989, 1992, 1998, 2001,2007, 2010, 2016 and 2019 do not move northeast or southwest.

In 1981, 1982, 1990, 1991, 1999, 2000, 2008, 2009, 2017 and 2018 do not move south or north.

The flying stars

The nine major planets of our solar system (not seen to scale). From the largest to the smallest, they are Earth, Jupiter, Saturn, Venus, Mercury, Neptune, Mars, Uranus and Pluto.

The flying stars – or nine star ki – is a system of oriental astrology derived from the I Ching. It helps to explain the fortunes of people and nations and to establish what are the best cures for each individual derived from the element relating to your date of birth (see the chart, opposite).

The universe moves in cycles where everything repeats itself down to the last stellar alignment which helps make things predictable. We know that if we get the same ingredients, mix them in the same fashion and then bake them in the oven at the same temperature for a certain length of time we are going to end up with the same result every time. Hopefully a perfect cake!

The planets line up in the same positions in regular cycles of movement. There are many cycles and cycles within cycles. There is one every 13,500 years, 25,800 years, 120 years, 81 years, sixty years, and nine years, and there are cycles that change every 24 days, 16 days and nine days.

Once these cycles have been monitored and learned from, they allow us to know what is going to happen. When they repeat themselves, the same things are going to happen. During previous cycles, for example, the Mayan and Egyptian architects were the best in the world, and the Greek mathematicians and the Roman inventors were the best in their field, but today no one would be interested in the latest Greek theory. These countries are poorer now, but the cycle will change again.

Everything on this planet goes through recurring cycles. Take a plant, for example. We know that it is going to go through five phases:

1 Seed
2 Sprout
3 Blossom
4 Fruit
5 Rot, then back to seed.

Identifying your element according to the flying stars

Each year starts in accordance with the oriental calendar which is around the 4 or 5 February

1901	Fire	1922	Metal	1943	Wood	1964	Fire	1985	Metal
1902	Earth	1923	Earth	1944	Earth	1965	Earth	1986	Earth
1903	Metal	1924	Wood	1945	Water	1966	Metal	1987	Wood
1904	Metal	1925	Wood	1946	Fire	1967	Metal	1988	Wood
1905	Earth	1926	Earth	1947	Earth	1968	Earth	1989	Earth
1906	Wood	1927	Water	1948	Metal	1969	Wood	1990	Water
1907	Wood	1928	Fire	1949	Metal	1970	Wood	1991	Fire
1908	Earth	1929	Earth	1950	Earth	1971	Earth	1992	Earth
1909	Water	1930	Metal	1951	Wood	1972	Water	1993	Metal
1910	Fire	1931	Metal	1952	Wood	1973	Fire	1994	Metal
1911	Earth	1932	Earth	1953	Earth	1974	Earth	1995	Earth
1912	Metal	1933	Wood	1954	Water	1975	Metal	1996	Wood
1913	Metal	1934	Wood	1955	Fire	1976	Metal	1997	Wood
1914	Earth	1935	Earth	1956	Earth	1977	Earth	1998	Earth
1915	Wood	1936	Water	1957	Metal	1978	Wood	1999	Water
1916	Wood	1937	Fire	1958	Metal	1979	Wood	2000	Fire
1917	Earth	1938	Earth	1959	Earth	1980	Earth	2001	Earth
1918	Water	1939	Metal	1960	Wood	1981	Water	2002	Metal
1919	Metal	1940	Metal	1961	Wood	1982	Fire	2003	Metal
1920	Earth	1941	Earth	1962	Earth	1983	Earth	2004	Earth
1921	Wood	1942	Wood	1963	Water	1984	Metal	2005	Wood

Even metal follows a predictable cycle:

1   Dust gets blown into a volcano

2   It then gets hot during a volcanic eruption

3   It cools down and solidifies

4   Pressure creates metal

5   The weather erodes it until it once again turns back into dust.

Every year, the energy on the earth is different. It is influenced by the gravitational pull, electrical fields, the solar system, the magnetic fields of the earth, volcanic eruptions or tempests and by man. The ancient Chinese eloquently said on this earth there is heaven's luck, earth's luck and man's luck. We cannot change heaven's luck, because we cannot influence the stars and the planets. However, heaven's luck can influence the weather to seem to be like spring all year round. But another year we might get a long, hot summer and during the next we might experience more rain than we have had for decades. These fluctuations are dependent upon which configurations are in the constellations. With knowledge, you can match up the cycles within the cycles and predict quite accurately what the weather will be like, how different people will react to different weather conditions, and how the fortunes of different countries will fluctuate. This is why the different societies of the world take it in turns to dominate.

The flying stars and us

We are in embryo for about nine months. During that time, we take in all sorts of energy, allowing us to develop at a phenomenal rate. Our bodies develop in a certain systematic fashion, the spinal cord first, then the heart, and so on. If a woman is pregnant during late autumn, winter and early spring, she will be eating predominantly winter food, like stews and soups. If she is pregnant during late spring, summer and early autumn, she will be eating salads and lighter food. Different foods strengthen different organs; if you have an upset stomach, soup is going to encourage the healing process, whereas greasy food like mackerel and chips won't. If you have a serious lung infection like bronchitis, mucous creating foods like dairy or a heavy stout are going to make it worse, whereas steamed green vegetables and rice will make you better. Likewise, the food a pregnant woman eats will help determine the strength of each organ of her baby.

The planets and seasons also strengthen and weaken different organs. If a person has a lung weakness, it can be worse during the damp of autumn. Also at this time of year, everybody will come under what the Chinese call a metal influence so they will tend to get projects finished, but can also tend to feel a little depressed. These are the negative and positive emotions stored in the lungs which is the most active organ during the autumn.

Someone who is born with a constitution of delicate lungs will find that during years which have an autumnal energy it will be more difficult to achieve goals. They will have less energy available since it will be used for healing instead. During this sort of a year, such a person would be advised not to take risks with health or finances. But if the lung (metal) energy was supportive, that person could expand without a care.

Someone who has a strong liver will be creative, changeable, spontaneous, flexible, easy going, full of ideas and fun. In the negative, they are bad tempered, aggressive and moody. As our bodies develop, some organs will be stronger than others because we have only received nine months of planetary configurations and seasons, we missed out on three months of the year. For further reading on this subject, see opposite.

Useful information

Useful addresses

For information about feng shui seminars and consultations, please contact:

The Feng Shui Company
Ballard House, 37 Norway Street
Greenwich, London SE10 9DD

Telephone/ Fax: 07000 781 901 or 0181 293 4471

Sarah Shurety teaches all facets of feng shui including Classical Landscape Form School, The Four Pillars of Destiny, Space Cleansing, The Compass School, Nine Star Ki and Feng Shui for Gardens from introductory to advanced levels.

Please contact either The Feng Shui Company or The Lucky Feng Shui Company (see address below) for information about personal, telephone or postal consultations for your home or business by Sarah Shurety or one of our qualified consultants.

To hear cures designed to bring Love, Marriage and Happy Relationships, more money and a wealth of other Feng Shui cures to benefit every aspect of your life telephone Sarah Shurety's Feng Shui Top Tips, on 0336 800188. Calls are charged at 50p per minute at all times.

Feng shui cures

All the cures mentioned in this book can be supplied by The Lucky Feng Shui Company including a wide range of books, wind chimes, mayan balls, purifying incense, bagua mirrors, flutes and fountains. Please telephone for a free catalogue:

The Lucky Feng Shui Company
Sunshine Cottage, Chedzoy
Somerset TA7 8RW

Telephone/Fax: 07000 781901

Further reading

An Anthology of the I Ching WA Sherrill and Chu (Routledge & Kegan, 1970)
Chinese Customs Henry Dore (Graham Brash, 1987)
Creating Sacred Space Karen Kingston (Piatkus, 1996)
Electromagnetic Pollution Solution Dr G Swartwout (Aerai Publishers, 1991)
Feng Shui and Western Building Ceremonies Derham Groves (Tynron Press, 1991)
Feng Shui for Business Evelyn Lipp (Times, 1989)
Feng Shui Made Easy William Spear (Harper Collins, 1995)
Outlines of Chinese Symbolism CAS Williams (Customs College Press, 1931)
Sacred Space Denise Linn (Rider, 1995)

The Astrology of the I Ching WA Sherrill and Chu (Routledge & Kegan, 1971)
The Book of Reincarnation and the Afterlife Lao Ng (Sashnon, 1928)
The Ki Steve Gagne and John Mann (Spiralbound Books, 1985)
The Ki - An Ancient Oracle Takashi Yoshikawa (St Martin's Press, 1986)
The Power of Place Winifred Gallager
Are you Sleeping in a Safe Place? Rolf Gordon (Dulwich Health Society, 0181 670 5883)
Ways to Paradise Loewe (Fakenham Press, 1979)

Acknowledgements

The publisher thanks the photographers and organisations for their kind permission to reproduce the following photographs in this book:

1 Elizabeth Whiting & Associates /Tom Leighton; 4-5 Getty Images /William J Herbert; 6 Gross & Daley; 9 Explorer /R Baumgartner; 10 Robert Harding Picture Library /Michael J Howell; 14 Arcaid /Belle /Earl Carter; 16 The Interior Archive /Chris Drake; 18 Getty Images /Rex A Butcher; 25 Camera Press /Christopher Simon Sykes; 27 Edifice /Gillian Darley; 28 The Interior Archive /Simon Brown; 30-31 The Interior Archive /Christopher Simon Sykes; 32 Robert Harding Picture Library /Fritz von der Schulenburg /c Country Homes & Interiors/IPC Magazines; 33 John Glover; 34 Gross & Daley; 38 Edificie /Philippa Lewis; 40 Clive Nichols /garden designer Jane Fearnley-Whitingstall; 41 The Interior Archive /Laura Resen; 42 Tim Street-Porter /designer Kathryn Ireland; 44 Gross & Daley; 45 The Interior Archive /Fritz von der Schulenburg; 48 Marco Ricca /Clodagh Design; 50 Belle Magazine /Simon Kelly; 51 The Interior Archive /Simon Brown; 54 The Interior Archive /Simon Brown; 56 Camera Press /Appel; 57 Abode/Trevor Richards; 61 Colin Walton; 62 The Interior Archive /Chris Drake; 63 Tim Street-Porter /interior designer Sandy Gallin; 65 Elizabeth Whiting & Associates /Tom Leighton; 69 Andrew Lawson; 70 The Interior Archive/Fritz von der Shulenburg (Stephanie Hoppen); 72 Colin Walton; 75 Pia Tryde; 76 Elizabeth Whiting & Associates /Jean-Paul Bonhommet; 77 Elizabeth Whiting & Associates /Simon Upton; 81-82 Elizabeth Whiting & Associates /Rodney Hyett; 83 Marco Ricca /Clodagh Design; 87 The Interior Archive /Fritz von der Schulenburg; 88-91 Simon Brown; 92 Edifice /Gillian Darley; 94 Andrew Lawson; 95 Jerry Harpur /garden designer Bob Dash, Long Island; 98 John Glover /garden designers Julian Dowle & Koji Ninomiya; 100 Elizabeth Whiting & Associates /Rodney Hyett; 101 Edifice /Philippa Lewis; 102 Clive Nichols; 104 Abode/Ian Parry; 105 Edifice /Philippa Lewis; 106-113 Colin Walton; 114 Michael Garland /designer Mimi London; 115 Colin Walton; 117 Ray Maine/Mainstream; 119 Andrew Lawson; 124 Science Photo Library /Magrath Photography; 131 Colin Walton; 132 Getty Images /World Perspectives; 136 Science Photo Library /Lynete Cook.

Index

ancestor area, 23-4
animals, as cures, 118-21

bagua, 18-29
  applied to the garden, 97
  areas of, 19, *19*
  relating it to your home, 20, *20*
  understanding, 19-20
bagua mirrors, as cures, 111, *112*
bathroom and toilet location, 85-6
bathrooms, 82-7, *82, 83, 84, 87*
  with good feng shui, 86-7
beams in bedrooms, 65
bedrooms, 62-75, *62, 63, 65,*
  66- 7, 69, 70
  location, 63
  with good feng shui, 71-4
beds:
  choosing and positioning, 64-5
  cleansing, 64
  different types, 69-70
  directions to point, 68
  for children, 77-9
benefactors area, 26

candles, as cures, 114, *114*
car:
  clutter in, 17
  using the bagua template, 29
career area, 21-2
ceilings in bedrooms, 65
Chaplin, Charlie, 133
chi and its different forms, 11-13
children area, 26-7
children's rooms, 76-81, *76, 77,*
  78, 81
  with good feng shui, 79-80
  position of, 76
Chinese temple, *9*
choosing a new home, 100-5
Classical Landscape Form School,
  see Form School
cleansing, 126-31
  procedure, 129-31
  the bed, 64
  what you will need, 127-9
  when to do it, 128
clutter, 8-13

colour as cures, 115-17
compass points, establishing, 135
Compass School, 18-19
consultations, 13
crystal in the dining room, *61*
crystals, as cures, 112-13, *113*

desk, positioning, 89-92
dining rooms,56-61, *56, 57, 58-9,*
  61
  position, 56-60
  with good feng shui, 60-1
direction of moving, 100-1
directionology, 132-5
directions, good for moving, 134
dragon veins, 10
dressing room, 64

elderly, rooms for, 74-5
  with good feng shui, 75
element, identifying, 137
energy bands, 132
entrances, 94-5
extended areas, 21

fame area, 28, 29
feng shui:
  in a child's room, improving, 81
  principles in the garden, 94
  schools of, 18
  what is it?, 8-9
five elements, 108-10
Fives, The, 135
fluorescent tube lighting, 114
flying stars, *136,* 136-8
Form School, 18-19
four-poster beds, 69
front and back doors, 41
front doors, 32-7, *32, 33, 34*
  direction facing, 35
  with good feng shui, 33-4
front gardens, 38-41, *38, 39, 40*
  with good feng shui, 40-1
Fu Hsi, 8, 19
futons, 69

garages, 43
gardens, 93-9, *94, 95, 96, 98*

with good feng shui, 97-9
Grand Duke, position of, 134

hallways, 41-3
  with good feng shui, 42-3
halogen lighting, 114
headboards, *65*
  different shapes of, 70
healing crystals, as cures, 113
heaven's chi, 11
heavy objects, as cures, 117-18
house name, 38
house number vibrations, 36

I Ching, 8, 10

kitchens, 50-1, *50, 51, 52-3, 54*
  with good feng shui, 51-5
knowledge area, 28

ley lines, 10
light, as cure, 113-14
lo shu, 8, 19
luo pan, 10

mayan balls, 111
  and cleansing, 129
metal beds, 69
microwaves, 55
mirrors, as cures, 111-12, *112*
mirrors in the bedroom, 71
missing areas, 21

new homes:
  auspicious signs, 103
  choosing, 100-5
  things to avoid, 103-5
nine basic cures, 108-25
numerology, 36-7

office with good feng shui, 92-3

plants, as cures, 121-2
predecessor chi, 12-13

relationship area, 22-3
revolving and moving things, as
cures, 124

round houses, *27, 105*

Saturn, 132, *132*
  annual position, 135
shiny objects, as cures, 111
sitting rooms, *8, 10,* 44-9, *44, 45,*
  46-7, 48, 100
  with good feng shui, 48-9
smudge stick, 128
  using, 129
sound, as cure, 115
staircases, 41
studies, 88-93, *89, 90-1*
summer houses, 95
surveying the plot, 10-11
symbols, as cures, 122-3

Tai Chi area, 25-6, *25*
television sets, 44-5
toilet lids, 82-3
toilets, 82-7
transcendental cures, 17, 125
trigrams, 8, *8*

Van Allen belts, 132

wardrobe, clutter in, 17
water beds, 69
wealth area, 24
wind chimes, as cure, 114-15, *115*
workshops, 43